The Adventu

Mary McManus, MSW

"We must let go of the life we have planned, so as to accept the one that is waiting for us." ~Joseph Campbell

To finding your bliss

Mary McManus

March 2019

Other books by Mary McManus:

Coming Home: A Memoir of Healing, Hope and Possibility
Going the Distance: The Power of Endurance
Feel the Heal: An Anthology of Poems to Heal Your Life

The Adventures of Runnergirl 1953 published by KDP

Table of Contents

Dedication and Acknowledgements

This book is lovingly dedicated to:

My husband Tom who has been by my side stride for stride for over 40 years. Here's to many many more adventures to come....

The earth angels who brought a touch of grace to my life and helped me to overcome my challenges.

My village who embrace me and surround me with unconditional love cheering me on to go the distance on the roads and in my life.

To anyone who was given a diagnosis and told what their limits would be....Remember you are not your diagnosis...You have the power within you to heal!

With deepest gratitude to Anthony Raynor for giving me an invitational entry to the Bermuda Half Marathon 2018. It gave me the opportunity of a lifetime to know that I am healthy, whole and healed.

Thank you to Race Directors Dave McGillivray, Paulie Collyer and Alain Ferry for giving me the opportunity to run my race at my pace.

Thank you to all the mind/body luminaries who lit the spark that led me out of the dark night of my mind, body and soul and led me into the light of how life is meant to be lived.

Introduction

"The best way to predict the future is to create it." ~Abraham Lincoln

Once I received the diagnosis of Post-Polio Syndrome, a disease deemed by Western Medicine Standards to be a progressive neuromuscular disease, I worked hard to live by Abraham Lincoln's philosophy and the philosophy of many luminaries of the New Age. In December of 2006 life as I had come to know it came to a screeching halt. I was not going to take the diagnosis sitting down.

Sometimes it feels as though life is going to crush us but then we have the opportunity to turn around and crush goals in life! At first I was afraid - very afraid and then I got still and asked for Divine Guidance. The answers came through my pen, what I came to call my divining rod for healing in the form of inspirational poetry; powerful words that inspired mind, body and soul to heal. I was creating my future; a future very different than the one the doctors predicted for me harnessing the power of my imagination to heal. I was told to prepare to spend the rest of my life in a wheelchair, and to anticipate an accelerated decline in functioning as I aged.

I traded in my wheelchair, leg brace and cane for a pair of running shoes. I went on to become an endurance runner. My adventures as runner girl 1953 (the year I was born) launched when I was 54 years old.

After writing my second memoir, "Going the Distance: The Power of Endurance," my friends encouraged me to write another book about my healing odyssey from the effects of childhood paralytic polio and severe childhood trauma. The theme of this book came to me during a run in August 2017. I knew I needed to take a broad brush look at my healing journey across over a decade of healing and to highlight the transformational and redemptive power of the sport of running. Through my running and life adventures my mettle was tested and friendships were forged to last a lifetime. In "The Adventures of Runnergirl 1953," I'll briefly take you back to when I contracted paralytic polio at the age of 5 and to receiving the diagnosis of Post-Polio Syndrome at age 53.

I'll answer the question, "How did you go from being told to prepare to spend the rest of your life in a wheelchair to the finish line of the 2009 Boston Marathon?"

You'll be inspired by my response to a major setback of a serious knee injury in December of 2014 that "they" said would sideline me from running for the rest of my days.

It's the 10 year anniversary of when I bought my first pair of running shoes; a perfect time to take a look back and share with you the adventures of this runner girl. In my quest to heal my life, I was led to the sport of running and found the treasure of myself along the way. Come along with me as I share the adventures of a lifetime after life as I had known it came to a screeching halt with the diagnosis of Post-Polio Syndrome.

From my heart to yours
In health and wellness
Mary McManus, MSW
January 2019

Never Tell Me The Odds

"Believe me, the reward is not so great without the struggle." ~Wilma Rudolph, Gold Medal Olympian and polio survivor

"Good evening ladies and gentlemen we are beginning our final descent over Boston...."

The sound of the Captain's voice receded into the background. As I looked out the window and saw the lights in the City below, I was reminded of how a poem I wrote in February of 2007, illuminated my way out of the dark night of my mind, body and soul.

Channel 7 Boston news story   **April 16, 2010**

Frances Rivera (TV news anchor): Well she could never play sports because of an illness and now she can run for miles.

Matt Lorch (TV news anchor): We're going to have the inspirational story of her 26 mile run through Boston.

Frances: This is something else. An inspirational run by a local woman.
Matt: How she went from walking with a cane to finishing the Boston Marathon.

Matt: Well we are just 3 days away from Marathon Monday and there will be plenty of inspirational stories in the 114th Boston Marathon.

Frances: One runner in particular from last year is hoping to help motivate people to lace up their sneakers this year. She was diagnosed with polio at age 5 but managed to run the Boston Marathon at age 55. The Night Team's Rhett Lewis has her story.

Mary: I was in a leg brace, using a cane and a wheelchair at times.

Rhett: Not for long. After years of suffering, Mary McManus decided she wasn't going to take Post-Polio Syndrome sitting down.

Mary: I want to be free in my body. I want to dance. I want to walk.

Rhett: With the aid of Spaulding Rehab and an angelic personal trainer Mary began to reach her goals. But she didn't stop there.

Mary: I said I have one more goal and she said what's that and I said I want to run the Boston Marathon.

Rhett: A daunting task for someone in perfect health Mary encountered her fair share of challenges.

Mary: I really had to overcome a lot not only physically but psychologically to know that I belonged among these people.

Rhett: After 13 months of agonizing training much of it in the brutal New England cold Mary McManus conquered her limitations and Heartbreak Hill crossing the finish line here on Boylston Street with her husband and daughter by her side.

Mary: When they heard I was going to do it they said well you're not going to be out there by yourself. And I said well you guys have never run a marathon. They said we don't care we're going to do it with you.

Rhett: Making the 7 hour 45 minute journey to the finish all the more memorable.

Mary: It was a moment of celebration. It was a moment of redemption the fact that here I was a polio survivor. I crossed the finish line of the Boston Marathon.

Rhett Lewis - 7 Sports

C-3PO is rattling off the odds while he stands over Han Solo's shoulder in Star Wars: The Empire Strikes Back. C-3PO has calculated the unlikely and grim odds of Han being able to avoid hitting an asteroid. Han Solo quips back, "Never tell me the odds."

The odds of becoming high school valedictorian after contracting paralytic polio and fighting for my life every night were quite slim. The odds of being selected for Alpha Sigma Nu, the Jesuit Honor Society at Boston College were quite slim. It took me 4 years to complete my Masters degree in Social Work. I nearly lost the use of my right arm due to a misdiagnosed staph infection and had a 6 week hospital stay.

I was told I shouldn't run again after a serious knee injury in December of 2014. What were the odds I would go on to run 3 consecutive Bermuda Half Marathons? It takes dedication, hard work, perseverance, fierce determination, strength and courage to beat the odds. At times, it was a messy and uncertain journey that required trusting The Force with all of my heart and soul.

The deck was stacked against me. Without warning, on June 3, 1959, I dropped to the ground in Kindergarten class. Three years after contracting paralytic polio, shortly after coming out of my leg brace, my father became alcoholic. Nine years of emotional, physical and sexual assaults followed until he died by suicide when I was 17 years old. In December of 2006 I was diagnosed with Post-Polio Syndrome and told to prepare to spend the rest of my life in a wheelchair.

In many ways, my life has been like an adventure movie. I battled evil, and fought for my life. Every time somebody told me I shouldn't or couldn't do something, I turned around and said, "Watch me now."

Never tell me the odds!

"Out of our deepest wounds we find our greatest strength, our most beautiful treasures and the knowledge that love is far greater, and more powerful than any experience we endure." ~Mary McManus

The buzzing hum from the fluorescent lights echoed the buzzing in my nervous system. I sat waiting for my first appointment at the Post-Polio Clinic at the International Rehab Center for Polio and Post-Polio. My complexion was as white as the paper that covered the exam table. I felt as fragile and vulnerable as that piece of paper that gets ripped off and tossed away after each exam. Every inch of my body hurt. I was exhausted. I was sick and tired of feeling sick and tired. I hadn't cared whether or not I woke up in the morning. My husband and twins needed me. Ironically, I was at the peak of my career as a social worker. I couldn't sleep. I felt depressed. My award-winning career as a social worker at the Department of Veterans Affairs no longer fueled my soul. Somewhere deep inside of me I felt there had to be a way out of the hell I was living in.

The symptoms began in 1996 with fatigue and burning muscles. I was anxious. At times, I noticed the limp from paralytic polio returned. In 1992 I had reconstructive leg surgery to correct the deformity of my left leg and to avoid a total knee replacement at the young age of 39 years old. I felt as though my body was deteriorating and my life was falling apart. In 2004 I told my primary care physician I was afraid there was something seriously wrong with me. I suggested the diagnosis of Post-Polio Syndrome.

Dr. Bailen sat behind his mahogany desk piled high with manila patient folders. He gestured for me to have a seat after conducting a thorough physical exam.

"Everything you are experiencing is emotional. Your EKG is fine, blood pressure, pulse rate are all fine. Post-Polio Syndrome simply doesn't exist. Maybe you're experiencing empty nest syndrome. {My twins had not left the nest yet.}"

He went into a closet and returned with a sample of Paxil.

"I'd like you to try this. And I'll give you a referral to see a psychiatrist. You're suffering from Post Traumatic Stress Disorder based on your history...."

I had been in and out of therapy for years. As a clinical social worker I knew PTSD was part of the problem but there was something profound happening in my body that needed medical treatment. I went home and flushed the Paxil down the toilet.

As I sat in my office between patients, I experienced my heart racing, difficulty swallowing, pain and tingling down my right arm, pain in my neck, and exhaustion that went deep into my bones. I dragged my body around with me. My thoughts raced. I tried to quiet them as I wrote patient notes.

"Should I go to an emergency room? Am I having a stroke or maybe a heart attack ... "

but the symptoms passed. I knew there was nothing acute happening to me. I met with my patients. I allowed the members of my team to vent and provided them with emotional support. On one level I functioned as a clinical social worker, an exemplary team member and being the most productive social worker in my department. On the inside, I was withering away. I was dying a slow and excruciatingly painful physical, emotional and spiritual death. I prayed to God I wouldn't wake up in the morning. I couldn't bear the pain of this existence any longer.

Guilt set in. How could I leave my family, my patients? I was suffering and wanted a way out. I never thought about suicide. I knew the pain of suicide all too well.

I prayed and asked for help.

The answer came to me. "Google Post-Polio Syndrome."

Just 30 minutes from my house, I found the Spaulding Rehab Hospital's Outpatient Clinic in Framingham.

Trembling I picked up the phone to take the first step on my healing journey back into life.

On May 25, 2007, I took a leap of faith leaving my award winning career as a VA social worker to heal my life without any idea of what that meant. I was three years shy of when I was eligible for retirement. As my husband Tom said, it was a no brainer for me to leave. Somehow the finances would all work out. Without my health what good would my life be if I continued to work. I vowed that if I could no longer serve my veterans and their families, I would leave.

I discovered the power of my pen, my divining rod for healing and as I created a future self without any limitations from the past through writing poetry, I began to heal mind, body and soul.

"There is no use trying, said Alice, one can't believe impossible things. I dare say you haven't had much practice, said the Queen. When I was your age. I always did it for half an hour a day. Why sometimes I've believed as many as six impossible things before breakfast." ~Lewis Carroll

On Guardian Angels and Earth Angels

As I lay paralyzed on the couch from the neck down, my mother glared at me while smoking a cigarette. I didn't know why she couldn't or wouldn't care for me. I had to wait until my father or grandfather came home to get my basic needs met. I had a vision of a Being with a long flowing beard who extended a hand to me only there was no physical hand. This Being sent a well bucket for me to climb in, and, although I was paralyzed, I was able to step into the well bucket to be reeled up to meet this Being. I felt safe, at peace and happy. Somewhere inside of me I knew that I had to make a choice. In that moment I made a choice to return to my physical body. Movement returned to my right side. I wiggled around a little bit on the couch; enough movement to hold my story book. Everywhere I looked whether my eyes were open or closed and even in my story book, I saw this Being. I had my guardian angel to help me through.

"Hi – I'm from the March of Dimes. I understand your daughter has polio. May I come in and see her?"

"Yes! Someone has come for me," I thought. She tenderly helped me down onto the carpeted floor.

"Let me see how you can move…Can you move from side to side? Can you roll over?" she gently asked me.

Although I couldn't roll over, she proclaimed "You're one of the lucky ones."

"Really?" I thought to myself. "This is lucky?"

But she was right. There were many children who were institutionalized and in iron lungs. There were many more children and adults who never regained movement after paralysis. Thousands died in the polio epidemics. I **was** one of the lucky ones.

As someone addicted to prescription pain medication, my mother did not have the capacity to care for me. I had my guardian angel and encountered my first earth angel. The March of Dimes sent a physical therapist to evaluate me. She talked in hushed tones with my mother after she lovingly placed me back on the couch.

"I found the best physiatrist in New York for you," my father proudly announced in early July. "You can start physical therapy soon."

Excerpt from "Running the Race":

Early summer 1959 my kindergarten year
everyone around me filled with nervous fear
despite the Salk vaccine hope polio would disappear
the polio virus crept right up and knocked me in the rear.

Dancing all around the gym feeling free just like a bird
I dropped to the ground just like a stone
and no one said a word.
The pain it was so searing-the diagnosis even worse
"It's polio" the doctor said...he was abrupt and terse.

Called one of the 'lucky ones' I had a 'mild case'
but with the other athletes I could never keep their pace.
Miss Holly physical therapist, curly hair and a warm, broad smile
it tempered the pain of being apart to walk I'd take awhile.

The office was decorated in dark mahogany. Red leather padded the chairs in the waiting room. Miss Holly, the physical therapist came out to greet us. We were brought in to meet Dr. Eugene Moskowitz. His starched white coat was in sharp contrast to his heart overflowing with compassion. He got right to work and assessed my functioning while measuring me for a leg brace. I mentally checked out and wondered if I would ever be able to return to ballet class. I allowed him to do whatever he needed to do to get my body to work.

Miss Patricia was a tall graceful woman who wore pink tights, a pink tutu and pink toe shoes. She wore a light perfume that reminded me of fragrant flowers in Spring. The mirrored room with ballet barres and polished wooden floor was my sanctuary away from my cold rejecting mother. Before class I carried my shiny patent leather Capezio tote that held my leotard, tights and black ballet shoes. My friends and I gathered in the anteroom with cubbies and giggled as we transformed into ballerinas. We eagerly ran into the classroom lining up with straight backs prepared to practice...

Miss Holly sat next to me in the waiting room and asked me to choose a Dr. Seuss book from the array of Dr. Seuss books spread out on the round coffee table next to my chair. My legs were outstretched; my left leg bore the hip to ankle metal leg brace inserted into my red polio shoes. My crutches were propped against the wall behind me. She read Dr. Seuss to me in the waiting room, led me into the treatment room and removed my leg brace. She placed heavy hot wool blankets on my legs. To this day I cannot bear to wear anything that is made of wool. As she coaxed my muscles and nerves back to health, she recited the first line from the Dr. Seuss book I had chosen (invariably "The Cat in the Hat").

"The sun did not shine it was too wet to play...now it's your turn."

"So we sat in the house all that cold cold wet day."

"I sat there with Sally....we sat there we two...your turn."

"And I said how I wish we had something to do..."

We would recite in tandem throughout the treatment. She was a physical therapist ahead of her time. I often wonder what inspired her to use the rhythm of the poetry to distract me from the painful treatments. She tenderly put my leg brace back on after she finished the treatment. She commended me on my courage as she wrapped her hand around my hand on my crutch, and led me into Dr. Moskowitz's office. He evaluated my progress, monitored me for scoliosis and gave me exercises to do at home. Picking up marbles with my toes was excruciatingly painful and difficult but even at my tender age, I loved the challenge of it all.

Life was very different when I left the safe space of Dr. Moskowitz and Miss Holly's office with abuse at home, and taunting and teasing of my peers at school. I immersed myself in school work and decided my body was something that I would have to tolerate and lug around with me through life. Dr. Moskowitz in all of his wisdom and experience in Rehab Medicine suggested I go to a day camp where the emphasis was on swimming. He knew the owners and the philosophy of Badger Day Camp. After one camp failure, he knew this would be a good fit for me.

With an Olympic size swimming pool and world class swimming coaches, Badger Day Camp provided me with rare wonderful memories of my childhood. Badger has turned out many Olympians throughout its 80-year history.

The end of camp Olympics are still the highlight of the summer for the campers. The first year I attended Badger I was happy to sit on the sidelines. I was learning how to swim and build strength in muscles severely compromised by polio. The counselors found ways to support me and help me feel included in all activities even though I had many physical challenges. I excelled in Archery and Riflery and easily racked up medals for my achievements. Counselors encouraged me to try new activities like the trampoline. With their physical and emotional support, I took risks in the safe and supportive environment of camp. As time approached to sign up for the end of summer Olympics at the end of my second year at Badger, Joseph J. Stetz, Jr. approached me about racing in the butterfly competition. He knew of my history of polio. I thought he was crazy to suggest such a thing to me. The butterfly? The most difficult stroke? I couldn't even jump off the racing block or do a turn. There were only two other campers in my division taking on the challenge of the butterfly. I was guaranteed a place on the podium. Joe would not take no for an answer and I couldn't say no to this 6'2" brown eyed god as seen through the eyes of a 10 year old. Yet I was also terrified to say yes.

"We are going to work on everything you need to get ready for race day. I'll work with you one on one."

His strong presence, patience and the confidence he had in my ability to compete and finish the race were a God send to my life. His individual attention and encouragement were a healing balm for the violence I endured every night.

I lived under the threat of "If you tell anyone about this. I will kill you."

The acceptance by counselors and the Badger community reminded me of who I truly was as a child of God worthy of respect and dignity.

Badger Olympics Day arrived. Joe helped to calm my nerves before the race reminding me of all we worked on together. We both knew I was going to finish the race. I surprised myself when I fearlessly jumped off the starting block feeling a sense of pride that I was racing. Joe told me to not look to my left or to my right but to focus on swimming my own race. I struggled through that final lap but I did it! Joe extended a hand and helped me get out of the pool. He gently put his arm around me as he led me to the medal stand. I proudly took my place on the medal stand. After the awards ceremony, I clutched and cherished my bronze plaque signifying my third place finish. There was no time on the plaque nor did the plaque state there were only three people competing in the race. I finished and I finished in third place.

Joe gave me his address accompanied with a warm hug on the last day of Camp. He encouraged me to stay in touch with him. I wrote to him about the medical challenges I experienced and he wrote back beautiful letters of support. He attended Downstate Medical College. We lost contact through the years. One day in December 2004, I was stunned to see his obituary in the Boston Globe. I worked as a psychiatric social worker at St. Elizabeth's Hospital where he was on staff as a cardiothoracic surgeon. He died at the age of 62 in a single car accident a few months after he retired. Joseph was only 21 years old when I met him but he was a soul far wiser than his years. His legacy of love, compassion and caring lives on in all whose lives he touched.

From his Boston Globe obituary:

He was described as "An old-school doctor who didn't mind giving patients a much-needed hug," according to Bernadette Trenholm, Dr. Stetz's personal administrator and close friend.

"Appointments were always as long as they needed to be with him. If the patients needed two hours, Dr. Stetz would give them two hours."

He qualified for the 1964 swimming Olympic trials in the butterfly, but chose to pursue a career in medicine. He forfeited his Olympic bid. I often feel his presence in my life. Joe instilled in me the seeds of being a champion. I could overcome my challenges. He taught me how to compete and the true meaning of what it means to be a winner.

From "Running the Race":

I always wore those 'special' shoes the kids they poked and teased
With no support and much abuse with childhood I wasn't pleased.
But put nose to the grindstone and learned all that I could
I couldn't kick a ball but my grades were always good.

Years went by and no more thought to polio did I give
I accepted the limp and everything else and decided my life I would live.
But symptoms of weakness and muscle pain did grow
I kept a stoic face hoping no one else would know.

Life no longer was my own I struggled through each day
Suffered in silence, isolated from friends-trying to keep depression at bay.
And with the grace of glorious God my world it opened wide
I discovered there was a Post Polio team and they were on my side.

Using wheelchair to travel, set limits on what I could do,
resulted in joy to realize I could live life anew.
Celebrated my body - creaks, groans and need for a brace
While in my mind I focused on winning a 10K race.

Sought out paths for healing and my spirit flew free
for the first time in life, I could truly be me.
The chains are gone and possibilities abound
I'm a tree with my roots planted firmly in ground.

I'm now off the sidelines, no need to sit and whine
So much gratitude fills my heart and love and beauty shine.
After all these years I can join the loving human race
I exceed all expectations and now I set the pace.

I called Dr. El-Abd my master magician. After looking at my cervical spine MRI, he said, "This is a slam dunk."

I was referred to him by the Spaulding Rehab International Rehab Center for Polio after being diagnosed with Post-Polio Syndrome.

"I believe a trigger injection will bring you some relief. Let me explain to you what I'm going to do. You have a bulging disc pressing on your nerve at C-6 in your cervical spine. This is what is causing the pain down your arm, the tingling in your face and those throbbing sensations in your gums and teeth. We do a trigger injection. First we inject numbing medication, which will bring you instant relief. We follow up with injecting steroids which will decrease the inflammation and bring you longer lasting relief. How long have you had this pain?"

"Oh at least ten years," I answered.

"Why so long? Why didn't you tell anyone about it?" Dr. El-Abd asked with compassion yet horrified I would allow myself to suffer for so long.

"Good question," I thought to myself.

I walked into the reception area of Spaulding Rehab in downtown Boston. I could see Dr. El-Abd in the distance in his blue surgical scrubs with a lead collar around his neck. The lead collar protected him from radiation from the fluoroscopy machine that allowed him to guide the catheter into my cervical spine. The medications are injected through the catheter. I filled out the questionnaire and took my seat in the waiting area trying my best to relax. I implicitly trusted Dr. El-Abd and knew I was on the right healing path but I would have given anything to not have to go through the procedure. Dr. El-Abd's hands were incredibly sure and skilled; his warm, compassionate and kind demeanor were just what I needed at this crossroad in my life. I tried to allow his confidence to pierce through my anxiety.

Once he injected the "numbing medicine" I could feel the pain stop in my upper arm. I cried with relief.

The nurse wheeled me into the recovery room where Dr. El-Abd met with me after dictating his notes.

"You were a model patient in there. After recovery from the second injection, I'll send you for intensive physical therapy. You need to regain your strength and mobility. I have a great physical therapist here. Is this downtown location convenient for you?"

"The VA Clinic is right down the street!"

"I have your records from the Framingham clinic Mary but I am going to need to do an assessment that specifically focuses on your upper body," Allison told me during our first appointment.

She had a warm smile. There was something compelling about her presence that let me know I was not destined to be on a course of a progressive illness. She inspired a desire to heal within me. As she massaged my cervical spine, her cool hands were in sharp contrast to the heat of the pain I experienced for the past 10 years. We moved through passive range of motion exercises. She wrapped an ice collar around my neck, and sat with me. She asked questions about how I was functioning in different areas of my life. She told me about adaptive equipment we could order to ease the stress on my already overtaxed muscles. After the session we set up 3 times a week therapy sessions.

"Take a deep breath and lift your hips," Allison cued as I lay on the physical therapy table.

"Now slowly lower down vertebrae by vertebrae. I want you to really concentrate on making that connection to your spinal column. Can you feel it? Move slowly. How does it feel?"

I lost my connection to my body after collapsing from paralytic polio. I had to dissociate from my body to survive years of abuse and torture. It was a strange experience to reconnect with my body, yet one that I hungered for. I wanted to find my way home and Allison was my first tour guide as she provided the map I needed to reconnect with myself.

The first day I walked into the outpatient gym and saw all of the equipment and machines I thought to myself, "I'm going to be able to do this. I can get stronger. I know it's not going to be easy. I know it's going to take time and I have to be extremely patient with myself."

I wanted to feel better and I wanted to feel whole. Three times a week we worked together using Pilates, isometrics, weight training and cardio-vascular exercise to bring my body out of its withered state.

"You have quite a talent," Allison said when I presented her with an original poetry card to celebrate her engagement.

We talked about my new found passion for writing poetry and how it opened a portal for healing and joy.

"By the way Mary, did the adaptive equipment I recommended for you ever get delivered to your office?"

"No and I keep following up with employee health, prosthetics and everyone I can think of."

"Look Mary. You need this equipment. We are working so hard together and you are making wonderful gains. But here's the thing. If you don't have the equipment and you continue to work at your job, there is no way you are going to be able to maximize the benefits of your therapy. I will be happy to write a letter of advocacy for you letting them know that if they don't provide you with the equipment, you are at risk for the progression of your disease and they will potentially have a worker's compensation claim to deal with."

There was no doubt about it. Allison was my earth angel.

"Come on," she said. "I want to show you something."

She took me into a room with a biofeedback machine. She showed me the effects of the stress on my body as we simulated my daily tasks of talking on the phone, writing notes, spending a lot of time on the computer doing research and fulfilling the administrative duties of a social worker. I was stunned by the results.

"This doesn't even take into account the emotional stress you experience on the job Mary. Please think about leaving."

Every day I thought about leaving my career. I reflected on the freedom I would feel once I no longer had the rigors of an 8-4:30 job, a commute and could dedicate myself to writing and healing my life. A friend of mine suggested I keep a 30 day journal creating my future life after I left the VA. Whenever I didn't have patients scheduled I did the exercises from my home exercise program, wrote poetry and wrote in my journal about my life after the VA.

The day before I terminated my employment at the VA was the day I "graduated" from physical therapy with Allison. Ironically, the adaptive equipment arrived on my last day. Allison was leaving Spaulding to work as a traveling physical therapist. I was on my way to write new chapters in my life. It was a tearful yet incredibly joyful goodbye.

Shortly after being discharged from outpatient physical therapy I met Janine Hightower through Herb Simmons. He knew Janine through his participation in the Cardiac Rehab program at Boston Medical Center. I was launching my business New World Greeting Cards, original poetry for every occasion. She was a member of BNI, a professional networking group. As we sat in my living room, she talked about BNI and the benefits of being a member of this networking group. As she talked, I wasn't focused on growing my business. My mind zeroed in on her sharing with us how she used BNI to promote her in home personal training business.

"You know I'm curious," I said to Janine. "Do you think you could help me? I was just discharged from Spaulding Rehab."

I went on to tell her about my journey.

"I don't know," she said "but I'd certainly be happy to set up an assessment with you."

I couldn't even pass the initial fitness assessment.

"You're way too young to not be able to get off of the toilet seat without holding on to the sink or to not be able to get off of the couch," she said to me.

It was a statement of fact without judgment. She spoke the truth about my deconditioned physical state. I signed on to work with her once a week in personal training. I had no idea what or why I was doing this. I did know that if I was going to be in pain, I'd prefer to feel the pain of recovery instead of the pain of decline. Janine held enough faith for both of us that I could come out of my leg brace and have a good quality of life despite the diagnosis and prognosis I received.

Janine's mantra for our work together was a quote from Henry Ford, "Whether you think you can or you think you can't, you're right!"

At my six-month evaluation in February, I made dramatic improvements in every area of the assessment. I had come out of my leg brace. I knew I was on a healing path.

"Let's write down your goals for the next six months," Janine said feeling proud and satisfied with my progress.

"Well I want to feel free in my body. I want to dance. I want to be able to walk outside and feel unencumbered when I take a walk."

Janine feverishly wrote down my goals, and we worked out a plan. She gathered up her belongings and had her hand on the door knob.

"Wait. I have one more goal."

Janine stopped and turned around.

"I want to run the Boston Marathon for Spaulding Rehab Hospital. I know they have a Race for Rehab team and I want to do it next year."

Did you ever have one of those moments when words fell out of your mouth after rising up from the depths of your soul without going through any thought process?

Janine was non-plussed. I don't know what kept her from turning tail and getting as far away from me as she could. She came back into my house, set down her things and without missing a beat said, "Well the first thing you are going to need is a pair of running shoes."

She laid out a cursory training plan and said that we would begin indoors to build up my cardio endurance. As soon as the weather got a little warmer, we'd go outdoors and I would learn how to run.

What had I just done?

Run Don't Walk   Neal Simpson Brookline Tab

While cleaning out the dormer in 2014, I came across the article we framed from the May 8, 2008 Brookline Tab.

Since she was a little girl, Mary McManus had rarely moved faster than a walk.

But last month, the former polio patient bought her first pair of running shoes. And now she's training for a marathon.

Paralyzed by polio at the age of 5, the Brookline mother of two now spends every day fighting back against the crippling effects of the disease that still threatens to rob her of her strength and mobility 50 years later. She said she won't stop until she runs her first marathon.

"I just know with every fiber in my body that we will," she said. "It's all happening."

McManus faces an uphill battle. Though polio itself has been virtually eradicated from the developed world, McManus is one of more than 440,000 Americans who could see a resurgence of symptoms decades later, according to the National Center for Health Statistics. Scientists believe this resurgence, called post-polio syndrome, is a result of natural aging and stress on the motor neurons that survive an initial polio attack.

Polio survivors learn to depend on these motor neurons as they recover, and can live relatively normal lives before they give out later in life, according to Mary Cole, a senior occupational therapist at the International Center for Polio in Framingham.

"There's usually a long period of stability," said Cole. "If not, there's something else going on."

Cole teaches post-polio patients how to save their energy, and recommends that many start using the braces and canes they once used as kids. "It's about improving quality of life," she said.

"A lot of people think exercise is what can get you through this, and that's not the case," Cole said. "Most of these patients have been overusing these muscles, and we need to find a balance."

But McManus said she refuses to slow down. She wants to prove that other post-polio patients don't have to, either.

"I'm here to let them know that that might be true for some people, but it doesn't have to that way," she said.

I was running to not only reclaim my life; to move out of a mindset of disability and emotional and physical paralysis. I was running to inspire others.

Readers commented on the on line version of the article.

DEAR MARY I'M SO PROUD OF YOU AND WISH YOU THE BEST OF THE BEST AT EVERY GOAL YOU ARE A GREAT WOMAN, I'M THINKING ABOUT MY LIFE IS A POST POLIO PERSON AND WISH I CAN DO THE SAME YOU DOING NOW
GOD BLESS YOU AND YOUR FAMILY
RAUL CORNEJO

Hello Mary, i stumbled onto your story.
I had polio when i was 14 months old; 27 years after, i still struggle with the physical and 'mostly' the emotional trials that accompany polio.
I'm a doctor so daily i encounter people with a variety of challenging conditions and i constantly draw strength from how different people embrace their unique situations.
I am particularly inspired by your unrelenting spirit, 50 years on!
I just got back from taking a long walk.
I was thinking about my life in general and saying to myself, are you just going to give in to polio without a fight?
I decided that i'll start running in the evenings to strengthen my calfs and increase my muscle bulk. During my walk, i also dealt with some emotional issues... but i digress.
I got home and got on the internet to see if there were any researched exercise routines beneficial to polio survivors, i wanted to be sure running was safe.
I got a lot of info, the unanimous advice was, don't over exert yourself, complete with the medical explanations why overexertion could be harmful.
I know running may be a stretch for me, i don't know how beneficial it will be, but i know that miracles still do happen.
Polio will not hinder me anymore. I am definitely gonna give it a shot.
I'll come back here to let you know my improvement.
I am very inspired by your determination and i thank you for sharing your story.
God bless you.

Hi Mary. I was listening to the radio the other night and I heard your interview. I don't know if you remember me but you took care of my husband George Murray while at the VA hospital as well as saving my life on a daily basis back then. You were truly my angel. I am so happy to have an opportunity to thank you for all you did for me back then and I have often wondered about how you were and then I heard you quite by accident as I still get up really early but the radio was on and I immediately recognized your voice. Do I think you will run this marathon, absolutely. You will do it. I am sorry you have gone through these health problems but you sound wonderful. I am going to get your book and I know I will love it. God bless you and I know he does.
Love
Maureen Murray

Maureen referenced my interview on The Jordan Rich Show on Boston's WBZ radio.

If you'd met Mary last year and then again today, you will be pleasantly surprised by the changes in her. She positively radiates with energy and good cheer. If exercise is how she's made the changes then I definitely want to start moving more too. It would be nice to have a follow-up after she has run her marathon.
Beth Blutt

I think it is awesome that she has been able to rebuild her strength a second time. I am encouraged now to continue exercising myself and continue to accomplish as much as I can in my golden years instead of settling for couch potato status.
Linda DuPre

The Starting Line

How does one go from a leg brace, a cane, and using a wheelchair at times for mobility to the starting line of the Boston Marathon, the world's oldest and most challenging marathon? I had no idea when I strapped on my cardiac monitor, a pair of sweatpants and my first pair of running shoes.

"We're going to do a run/walk sequence as a way of introducing your body to running," Janine told me as we went out the front door of my house to teach my body how to run.

"It's just a little quicker pace than walking," she said. "I know you've been watching Forrest Gump. Just imagine how that feels in your body."

My heart rate went up over 170. I thought my heart would jump out of my chest but I had to focus on my goal. I was taking the first steps on the road to my Boston Marathon.

Corrib Pub Run   June 1, 2008

It was a hot and humid day. I had incredible butterflies not knowing what to expect from my first 5K. It was a friendly neighborhood race that accepted all paces. Proceeds from the race benefitted neighborhood charities. Before the race we stood next to a couple and struck up a conversation. I learned that it's a common practice to strike up conversations with strangers at a road race. They were inspired by my story and wished us well as we parted ways at the starting line. I had to pinch myself to realize I, Mary McManus, aka "Easy Out Alper" was toeing the starting line for a road race.

As we ran through the streets of West Roxbury, Tom shouted, "First road race ever. She's a polio survivor!"

People cheered and I ran through the hoses that people sprayed the runners with to keep us cool. I experienced a sense of play and freedom that I'd never known before in my life. Each step was a challenge for me especially the last long hill. I hadn't run for more than 40 continuous minutes in my training program. I had only been running outside since late April. But it didn't matter. I was on the road to the Boston Marathon and this was my first time being cheered rather than jeered as I ran. I had to stop and walk after 40 minutes but once I approached the finisher's chute, Tom and I held hands sprinting together across my first finish line!

Using wheelchair to travel, set limits on what I could do,
resulted in joy to realize I could live life anew.
Celebrated my body- creaks, groans and need for a brace
while in my mind I focused on winning a 10K race.

Labor of Love   November 4, 2008

I had this aha moment as I inspected my feet. I looked at my big purple toe nail on my left foot and the blood blister on my right foot.

22

"Oh my God. What's happening to my body is like what happened when I was pregnant. It's going through changes at lightning speed. While I feel spiritually and physically fully alive since I started running, there are aches and pains and things happening to my body that never happened before."

Rather than putting on the pounds, they are shedding like magic! I have what is called a contracture on my big left toe. It's a small reminder of polio; the toe stays in a crooked position. As I was increasing miles, and forgot to keep my toenails trim, it took a real pounding. I feel like a real athlete now because I have to tape the toe before my run. A blister kit allowed my body to heal naturally and continue running without missing a beat. There is new life and transformation growing within me. This is a remarkable labor of love. I don't mind the aches and pains or the blisters because I am on a mission. I am stretching and growing in ways that were impossible for me before I said to Janine, 'Do you think you can help me get off of a low toilet seat?'

With Janine's loving guidance, I trust in the body's natural healing process and pay loving attention to what my body is telling me. I am blessed to be surrounded by love and to let in the most glorious love of all from Source. I am learning to love myself and take exquisite care of my body for the second time in my life. The first time was when I was pregnant with twins. Is this selfish? You bet it is and I highly recommend it. I am paying attention to nutrition and sleep, managing stress and taking time for meditation each day. The body is the temple which holds our sacred self.

There is the air of expectation I experienced when I was pregnant. What will it be like on Marathon Monday as I stand in the corral waiting for the starting gun to go off? Just like when I went into labor, I will shut out all distractions. Spirit will take over mind and body as I will focus on a single goal. I will feel the rush of tears, joy and exhilaration when I cross the finish line where loving arms await to embrace Team McManus. I am overflowing with gratitude for this amazing journey!

As humans, we all share those moments of doubt and fear questioning if we can achieve our goals. I knew that God spoke through me when I told Janine that my goal was to run the Boston Marathon to raise money for Spaulding but there were times when I wondered, was that really God's Voice I heard? Am I really supposed to be doing this? Is this my life's purpose at this moment in my life? After a run like The Tough Ten Mile Turkey Trot in the freezing cold with challenging hills, I know that Source within me moves me. I transcend my physical body and run from my heart and soul.

But every once in awhile, a little nagging voice asks, "How are we ever going to raise $9,000? How am I ever going to run 26.2 miles?"

And then, God answers in strange and delightful ways.

I had errands to run at Cleveland Circle; a turning point on the Boston Marathon course. After going through the hills in Newton and passing through Boston College, runners turn onto Chestnut Hill Avenue. Once runners get to Cleveland Circle, it is a straight shot to Kenmore Square with just a few small hills along the way. It's only 4 miles to the finish line from Cleveland Circle. Those little inner critics were chatting away. I dismissed them. My passport was no longer valid to travel to the land of negativity. I walked along Beacon Street to Boloco to get lunch to go.

"Excuse me. Do you have any spare change?"

I handed him a dollar bill.

After coming out of Boloco I noticed that the man who asked for money had gone. I looked down 'for some reason' and on the ledge of the Citibank there was change spread out. I picked it up. I knew it was for me.

It was hot from being out in the sunshine. When I got home I counted it. There were 5 quarters, 14 pennies, 3 nickels and 2 dimes. Five quarters is $1.25; 26.2 by adding the 1 and the 5 and scrambling the numbers a bit. We were scheduled to run 14 miles, 15 miles and then eventually 20 miles for our long runs. God was letting me know we have everything we need to go the distance in miles and for our fundraising!

24

Seventeen Miles or 119 Times Around the Track   January 11, 2009

This past week I trained outside in cold and wind, snow and ice but yesterday, it was 5 degrees with the wind chill. There was no reason to try to brave those elements for a 17 mile run. We went to the BU Fit/Rec Center. As people passed us around the track, the little polio part of myself thought, 'I'm not fast enough.'

"I can no longer be a slave to my past. I am running my own race. Each training run is an opportunity to learn more about myself, mind body and spirit; every race where I finish 'last' reminds me to celebrate who I am; to celebrate my courage, faith, determination and to let go of arbitrary measures of success."

I learn so much about myself during these training runs. There certainly is enough time for reflection with no distractions of the computer, phones, text messages or social media. I got in touch with the feelings of what it was like to feel powerless in my body juxtaposed with the strength and power I feel when I run. Strength and power had been taken from me when I collapsed on the gym floor when paralytic polio overtook my body and when my father and grandmother abused me. Yet the strength and power of God was always with me deep in my soul. I feel that strength and power every time I lace up my running shoes and go out on a run! Before I started running, I was terrified to feel my own power and strength. I thought I would want revenge. I thought the anger would consume and destroy me. I instead discovered the most powerful feelings one can experience are the power of forgiveness and God's great Love. The power of Love washed through me during yesterday's training run much like dialysis to remove the toxins of anger, shame, fear, doubt and feeling less than. Love is the most powerful source of purification. It is a blessing to be able to feel this Love. I felt this Love while my body pounded the track. It is time to forgive them for truly, they knew not what they did and to create new feelings, new memories on every level; to open wide to all that life has to offer.

Heartbreak Hill for the First Time   January 24, 2009

This morning at 8 am as we had the cooler packed and ready to go around Jamaica Pond, I felt God speak to me and I listened. "Go to Marathon Sports and get a route from Domenick D'Amico. It's time to get out on the Marathon Course!"

We had about 15 minutes to fill up water bottles, pack clementines and Power Gel into our pockets and get down to Marathon Sports before the group run took off. I felt in every fiber of my being we were meant to do this today!

We walked into the conference room at Spaulding Rehab Hospital. Blue gift bags adorned with matching blue curly ribbon were placed at each of the spots in front of the 14 seats around the conference room table. My breath caught as I reflected on how this moment compared to when I walked into Spaulding for my first cervical spine injection or when I hugged my beloved physical therapist goodbye.

The Development Team welcomed us to the first Team Meeting of Spaulding's Race for Rehab 2009 Boston Marathon Team. We were asked to introduce ourselves and say what inspired us to become a member of the Race for Rehab Team. I was overcome with emotion as I briefly shared my journey.

After everyone shared their journey we heard, "Hi! I'm Domenick D'Amico and I'm your trainer for the Team. It's my job to get you to the starting line healthy and to the finish line with a smile."

When we arrived at the store, Domenick was there along with other members of Marathon Sports Run Club. Team McManus was a wee bit nervous not knowing what to expect or what was going to happen today. He was deep in thought about what route we should run today.

"Have you run outdoors? Have you done hills?"

As we shook our heads and said, "Yes!" Domenick wrote out our 17.5 mile route on the back of a map. He narrated the route as he scribbled.

"You're going to go outbound on Beacon Street to Newton Wellesley Hospital, over to Wellesley, up Concord Road, over to Route 30 via the Marriott, down Route 30 through Heartbreak Hill, through BC to go around the Reservoir and then back to Marathon Sports."

I won't lie! It was not easy! If it were easy everyone would do it right? We didn't know where we were going. We had to watch out for black ice and gingerly navigate our way through snow and slush. When Tom set a pace that challenged me, I vacillated between feeling sheer exhilaration and dealing with demons from polio days. BUT we did it! Four hours and 45 minutes after we left Marathon Sports, we returned to a jubilant staff. This polio survivor ran Heartbreak Hill - all of it! I felt God's palpable presence with each step I took. We did a 17.5 mile run today including Heartbreak Hill. I felt Johnny Kelley's spirit blessing us whisking us along our first training run on Heartbreak Hill.

Two weeks before our first run on Heartbreak Hill, we returned from Puerto Rico, after a brief hiatus from the never ending brutal New England cold weather. On the plane ride home, we met Tom Kelley and his wife, Dottie. We shared the story of Team McManus not knowing the names of the people with whom we shared pleasant conversation to pass the time on the flight back to a snowstorm in Boston.

"Hi there...my name is Tom Kelley. My uncle was Johnny Kelley."

"I'm Dottie." "It's so nice to meet you."

"Johnny Kelley" I thought to myself. "As in **the** Johnny Kelley. Olympian and Boston Marathon champion through the decades?!"

Dottie shared with me that Tommy lives with Parkinson's Disease but he keeps on running as best he can. Running is his therapy. She asked for our mailing address. They had something they wanted to send to us. I had goosebumps all over.

As we parted ways heading to baggage claim, Dottie said, 'Good luck with the rest of your training! Come see us at the Expo at Packet Pick up. Remember, Johnny will be watching over you."

"Thank you. Get home safely and we'll definitely come see you at Packet Pick Up. You sure made my day!" I said with a broad smile and a full heart.

A week later a package came in the mail with a note written in Dottie's perfect cursive handwriting dictated by Tommy:

This is a poster created by Adidas for the 2004 BAA Marathon. I had Johnny sign a few when we roomed together at the Copley Plaza that week, and I know he would have gladly signed one for your family if he were here. Perhaps it will inspire you to run a good race, especially the last 6 miles. Johnny was an inspiration to many of us amateur runners and he lives on in the memories of countless runners. You can get a copy of his book Young at Heart on Amazon I believe. You'll note that his forefathers came over to the USA on the SS Marathon!!! Keep on running as I do. We loved your website and maybe some day we can meet again.

Young at Heart   January 29, 2009

Fairy tales can come true, it can happen to you
If you're young at heart
For it's hard, you will find, to be narrow of mind
If you're young at heart ~Rodgers & Hammerstein

"Young at Heart" is the title of Johnny Kelley's autobiography and the song played when they dedicated his statue on Heartbreak Hill in Newton. Ever since meeting his nephew, I researched Johnny, feeling that his presence is blessing our journey. Young at heart had special meaning for me during today's training run. As Janine ran by my side, she told me about her 70 year old client who celebrated the fact it was easier to get off of the toilet seat and stand. When Janine did my assessment, and I told her what functional areas I struggled with, she said to me, "Those are struggles for somebody in their 70's, not for someone who is only 53 years old."

The other day I cleaned out my attic, I found the tub chair I used because I did not have the strength or energy to stand in the shower. I scanned the attic to see my black polio shoes, toe up leg brace, wrist brace to ease the painful symptoms of carpel tunnel syndrome and what I once considered my swanky blue cane with its ice gripper. I confidently put them out on the sidewalk with a sign "Free"! I am a walking miracle. This is a journey of physical, spiritual and psychological transformation.

Fairy tales can come true and it's all happening to me. In just a few short weeks, I will be at the starting line of the 113th running of the Boston Marathon. I am clearing out the mental, physical and emotional blocks as they arise to have a wonderful path to the starting line. I am learning to temper fears by allowing the love of God to wash over my soul. I am fearless. I have my eyes on the prize. We move toward our fundraising goal of over $9,000 and I inspire so many with my story. I imagine how it is going to feel to get my medal and wear my jacket after I cross the finish line. I drink in every experience along this journey finding the lessons and the blessings in the triumphs and tribulations along the way.

From Hyannis to Hopkinton - Getting Ready!   February 23, 2009

This weekend I found myself in the Hyannis Resort and Conference Center milling among hundreds of runners wearing BAA Marathon jackets, buying running gear and feeling totally out of place. It was a miracle that I heard my cell phone ring above the din in the Conference Center.

"Hey ma it's me. I was doing a delivery for TJ's. My CD was skipping so I put on the radio. It was tuned to WERS and guess what I heard at the moment I turned it on?"

My son worked for TJ's Vegan House of Pizza. It was a collective pizza shop that suited his political views.

"What?" I asked absolutely stunned that he would call me like this.

"It was an advertisement for your A Cappella benefit concert for Spaulding! I just had to call to tell you. Have a great weekend and a great race on Sunday!"

"Thank you so much Autumn. That phone call really gave me a boost. I was feeling really nervous and to be honest a little out of place among all these seasoned runners."

"You're gonna do great. See you when you get home on Sunday."

We had lunch at Bogey's, the hotel restaurant. Since we were first timers, our waitress highly recommended an appetizer of green beans which were coated and fried. We had tuna sandwiches for protein, and French Fries to carbo load. We made sure to eat a lot of fruit throughout the day that we brought with us and were mindful to hydrate. After lunch it was off to pick up our bibs and free swag at my first ever Running Expo. We got to meet Dick and Rick Hoyt. I shared my story with Dick. He was inspired by my journey on the road to Boston.

As we watched TV and relaxed for the rest of the afternoon, I got the feeling that I should call Tim aka Derv Doiron who I met on line in the runner's forum, "Just Finish."

"Hey Derv," I said. I just wanted to wish you luck on your run tomorrow."

"Wow your timing is really something. I'm here to pick up my bib."

I hurried down to the lobby and worked my way through the crowds at the Expo.

"We couldn't get a room here," Derv said so we're staying about a mile and a half away. "Are you excited for the race tomorrow?"

"I'm excited. Nervous. You name it. I know we have the distance but I've never been in a race like this before."

He gave me a big bear hug and told me I'd be fine.

"It's so awesome to meet you in person," I said.

He inspired me with his journey. He began running just a year ago and is also going to run Boston. He overcame health challenges of diabetes and high blood pressure with a vigilant approach to taking care of himself. He got the nickname "Derv" from whirling dervish!

"I'd like to introduce you to my wife Deborah and my son Alex," Derv said.

"It's great to meet you!"

"I love to run with Wii Fit," Alex proudly said.

We chatted for a few minutes before Derv picked up his bib and headed back to his hotel.

"See you at the finish line!" we said to each other.

We signed up for the pre-race Pasta Dinner where I introduced myself to Race Director, Paul Collyer. I emailed him before we registered for the race to make sure it was an all paces race. He assured me and then reassured me that I would be fine as long as I finished before the last marathoner crossed the finish line. The marathon consisted of two loops and he used the same finish line for both races. He was happy to meet me and wished me well on my race.

The ballroom with dozens and dozens of round tables covered with white tablecloths set up for 20 people at each table was filled. The sound of chatting runners matched the sound of forks clinking against china. We did not know a soul in the room. We chose one of the few tables where there were vacant seats. We had a delightful conversation with three siblings who had a close loving family. As we served ourselves pasta, salad and Italian bread, I felt the butterflies flutter again in my stomach. I was about to embark on my first 13.1 mile road race. That's half a marathon! I ate mindfully taking in every moment of the pre-race atmosphere. The conversation quelled as Paulie stood at the podium getting ready to introduce running greats Bill Rodgers and Frank Shorter. I quickly learned there is no separation between everyday runners and running greats. I was enthralled with their running stories and tips for our races. They quipped with each other in tongue in cheek trash talk banter. After their talk we were invited to meet them. We had photo ops, a Boston Marathon poster signed by both Frank and Bill and I received words of encouragement as I prepared to run my first half marathon race on the road to Boston.

As I drifted off to sleep, I reflected on all of my blessings and was in awe of this new community called "runners."

It became overcast at gun time but the temperature was moderate as we crossed the starting line. We were in the 14 minute/mile pace corral just in front of the walkers. We took off at a fast pace - a 13 minute/mile pace. I told myself to release all feelings of lack and limitation and go with the flow. This was a training run so I needed to push my pace while I also monitored my heart rate. By mile 10, I abandoned my fueling and hydration plan. Sleet pelted my face and my only goal was to cross that finish line.

The post-race reception included bagels, peanut butter, bananas, hot soup from the 99 Restaurant, orange slices and water. I was shivering when I came into the ballroom. Among the thousands of runners streaming into the ballroom, Frank Shorter spotted me.

He put both of his hands on my forearms, looked at me straight in the eye and said, "I have no doubt you are going to finish Boston!"

I told him I wasn't feeling so well.

"Get hot soup and hydrate," he said while he congratulated me on finishing the race in tough conditions and signed my bib.

Although I wasn't feeling well, and should have gone upstairs to take a hot shower, there was a reporter interviewing runners. I told him my story and I was in the next day's Cape Cod Times:

Mary McManus, 55, of Brookline completed her first half marathon after making a remarkable recovery from a life-long battle against post-polio syndrome.

She spent time at the Spaulding Rehabilitation Hospital and began running just last February. She competed in her first race in June 2008, finishing a 5K.

"It's like having a new lease on life," said McManus, who ran yesterday's half marathon with husband Tom. "I was limping my way through life, but then decided to do something about it."

It was a phenomenal weekend; the first of many weekends that would come to be known as Camp Hyannis. I earned my first of many medals for finishing a race but the greatest prize was the friendships forged at the pre-race pasta dinner.

With just 8 weeks to go, I began to anticipate toeing the starting line of the 113th Boston Marathon.

Twenty Miles   **March 13, 2009**

One year ago, when we took our training outdoors, I ran for 30 seconds and walked for 4.5 minutes. Janine introduced me to hill training in late April. After I protested that I wasn't ready to run up a hill, she told me that I had better get used to it.

"After all Mary you're not training for just any race. You are training for THE Boston Marathon and you know you're gonna have to be ready to tackle those hills."

My heart rate would go up to 163 from an easy jog. Here I sit after being out in the freezing cold for over six hours having run and power walked TWENTY MILES!!! Starting out at 10 am the mercury hit all of 16 degrees and then there was the wind chill.

32

I saw the temperature and decided to just ignore it. The cold is the arch enemy of a person who suffered from Post-Polio Syndrome but I am a new me in a new world and so, it was time to prepare for the run. Our event coordinator suggested we start our long run at 10 or 10:30 to simulate Marathon Monday. I had my toast, juice, water and then oatmeal. Before we left at 9:45, I ate a banana and half a bagel with more water as I will in the Athlete's Village on Marathon Monday.

We got to Marathon Sports around 10 am. We did a long warm up since it was freezing outside and then decided we needed to power walk instead of run. We have done intensive training with a half marathon race, followed by a 19 mile long run within the week, speed drills and hill training. We had done a 15 minute/mile pace for 15 miles last Saturday and done cross training on the bike as well as speed drills on the track. If we were going to survive 20 miles in the cold, we had to pace ourselves. There was no reason to risk an injury now!

We were grateful for the sunshine but not thrilled about experiencing headwinds coming AND going. This was a training run in every sense of the word as we went farther and braved the cold longer than we ever had. We came, we power walked and we conquered feeling mentally and physically strong as we count down to Marathon Monday. I took two Advil tonight. I have not used Advil since last April when our training began to 'intensify.' Ha - I had no idea what intensify meant. With our longest training run in the books, we turned our attention to An Evening of A cappella Music to Benefit Team McManus' Spaulding Rehab Boston Marathon Run. The finish line of training and fund raising was in sight!

Getting a Head Start   March 19, 2009

No one ever suggested to this polio survivor that I could or should get a head start when playing tag, hide and seek or having to run and participate in gym class. I learned how to hold my head up high and maintain my dignity despite the ridicule and teasing I endured.

I shared my anxiety about being able to finish the Boston Marathon in under six hours with Domenick at a fundraiser for a fellow marathoner.

"Didn't anyone talk with you about getting an early start?"

"I thought about it when we first started training but I thought I didn't meet the qualifications."

"Let me email Barbara at the BAA and get this taken care of for you."

Because of my diagnosis, I was eligible to start with the mobility impaired runners. All I had to do was get a letter signed by my physician. Despite Dr. Rosenberg's belief that if I used it I would lose it, and the admonitions he issued with cautionary tales about setting limits as a survivor of paralytic polio, he had the letter ready for me when I drove out to Spaulding. Driving out along Route 9 to Framingham from our home in Brookline, I reflected on this miraculous journey from being fitted with a leg brace, and all the things I was unable to do when I first presented to the clinic. I reflected on the items I was prescribed to manage all the symptoms I experienced that had been left on the curb, to now picking up a letter to get an early start to run the Boston Marathon.

It is the grace that I have an early start. It's going to make a tremendous difference in terms of fatigue. Getting there and getting started will enable me to take full advantage of my peak energy time. Rather than having to wait two hours to cross the starting line, we'll be out on the course running with the pack. I will be able to enjoy Marathon Monday knowing that at last I have a head start.

I was fully prepared to push myself and start with the pack and somehow finish the course in six hours. Domenick believes that we may even finish in under six hours.

"You'll be so well rested from taper time and the energy of the crowds are going to carry you along," Domenick told me before our 7 mile taper run.

"What happens when the crush of runners catches up with us or when the wheelchairs pass us, do we step over to the side of the road?"

He was stunned by my question. "You have a right to be on the road just as much as any other runner or wheelchair participant."

Domenick blessed me and said, "You have put in all the work to train. You run your own race and have the experience of a lifetime. And remember I'll be waiting for you on Heartbreak Hill!"

Thanks to Domenick, I **will** be able to have the experience of a lifetime because, for the first time in my life, I am on a level playing field.

Ode to Marathon Training

Blisters, black toes, aches and pains
a change in my routine
Long training runs, the hills, the sprints
keep running clothes fresh and clean.
Carbo load and plan each meal
power gels and gatorade
no matter what the weather
no time to be afraid.
Humid – hot or freezing cold
snow against the face
wind or sun or raining
those running shoes I must lace.
What mile is this how long we been out
check heart rate drink H20
meltdowns joys and triumphs
only a few more weeks to go.
Heartbreak Hill won't break my heart
this year has been the best
found myself and made new friends
I feel incredibly blessed.

Our Last Long Run

Yesterday was our last long run before running the Boston Marathon. For 21 miles, we ditched iPods and wanted to simulate Marathon Monday. The day started out as cloudy and cool. Since it is the end of March, we layered with a short sleeve shirt, a long sleeve shirt and a jacket. We arrived at Marathon Sports to join the running club.

Using his signature hand gestures, Domenick explained, "21 miles will take you to the gates at Wellesley College. Turn around and run the same route you ran for the past several weeks."

In the spirit of trying to get everything organized the night before our last long training run, I made my husband's coffee in the coffee maker. Big mistake! He couldn't drink the coffee - yes it was that bad. We'd gone several miles when Tom slowed to a power walk. He was wilting right before my eyes. That was highly unusual for him. I relied on him to be our pacer. I got concerned.

"I'm feeling sluggish and my body is telling me to take it easy."

"Okay," I said, "but maybe this has something to do with you not having your usual cup of morning coffee."

He went into Starbucks and after drinking a large cup of coffee, he was back to his old self.

The sun broke through the clouds. By the time we got to Wellesley we needed to strip off layers of clothing. There were runners coming in from Hopkinton to Boston College who knew me by name. I recognized a few of the runners, but there was a mystery runner who I could not place. He called me by my name.

"Do you know who that was who cheered me and called out my name?" I asked Tom.

"I don't know. I thought you knew him," Tom replied.

I wondered if perhaps he was an angel. He vanished right after we saw him. When we arrived at the Reservoir at Cleveland Circle, a stiff wind kicked up and we had to don the layers we had shed; a good lesson for Marathon Monday. Do not throw our clothing into the street. We may need it for later in the day. We practiced our pacing and fueling. By the time we arrived back at Marathon Sports we knew with absolute certainty that Team McManus was ready for Marathon Monday.

Today we drove out to Hopkinton and traced the Marathon route. We had run from Natick to the finish line. We needed to get a visual of the route from Hopkinton to Natick as we mentally prepare for the Marathon.

It's all mental preparation now as we head into taper mode.

We are poised and ready to board the bus for the ride to Hopkinton and to have the time of our lives on April 20, 2009.

Six Sense Our Last Training Run   April 11, 2009

I did not misspell cents. I found a penny and a nickel on our last training run today. The nickel was right outside of Marathon Sports on Beacon Street where I began my journey of transformation from polio survivor to athlete. We ran from Marathon Sports to Hereford Street.

Domenick planned out the route for us. He said, with a punctuating gesture of his forefinger, "Do NOT go into the tunnel. Save that AND crossing the finish line for Marathon Monday."

On our return trip to the store, I thought I saw a penny and went to pick it up. It turned out to be an old piece of gum; round, flat, and without my glasses it looked like a penny. But a little farther down the street, there *was* a shiny penny.

I got lost in my own thoughts. "Six cents. Let me check the dates to see if they have any significance. 1994-2001. Wow that's seven years. I know seven is a mystical number - cool."

And then it hit me - Six Cents - Sixth sense.. I heard Obi Wan Kenobi say to Luke Skywalker, "Trust the Force Luke."

Even though I had a clear sign to let go and Trust, I had a serious case of taper madness. I focused on road closures. Of all things one can fret about a week before a Marathon I was afraid I was going to miss the bus out to Hopkinton. Our events coordinator sent out an email with meticulous details about Marathon logistics. If there were going to be road closures, would she tell us that we could drive to Spaulding where the bus leaves at 6:30 am? Of course not but the fear drove me. I checked in just to make sure that we would be able to get there by car. Even after I received email confirmation from the Vice President of Development that Storrow Drive would be open and there are no road closures at that time in the morning, I searched the internet for the list of road closures. I observed myself behaving in this maniacal fashion. I smiled. Taper madness in someone with a trauma history do not go well together. Finally, in my exhaustion, I turned it over to God. When I shared my case of pre-race nerves with Domenick, he reassured me that at that time the only street we cannot go down is Boylston Street.

Marathon Monday

It's Marathon Monday, it's my day to shine
with husband and daughter poised at starting line.
I know I can do this - there's no way to fail
tethered to God through this race I can sail.

For over a year, we've trained from our heart
mind, body, spirit - we're ready to start.
We know the course and we know the terrain
we're primed for the challenge - we know they'll be pain.

The glory's far greater than what we may face
we're living examples of God's shining Grace.
Shake out all the nerves - there's nothing to fear
let in all the love from the crowds as they cheer.

With prayers and angels our feet feel so light
joy overflowing the finish in sight.
We conquered the course fueled by love in our heart
the race had been won blessed by God from the start.

Boston Marathon Race Report   **April 22, 2009**

When I look back to April 2007, I was still wearing a leg brace and using a cane. When I look back to April 2008, I could not run for more than a minute. I remember running on Eliot Street toward home just for a minute and feeling as though I were really pushing myself.

Janine asked me a very powerful question, "How are you going to handle it when the going gets tough during the Marathon?"

I remember seeing my heart rate at 168 from just a minute of running. That was a far cry from the hill training we had done in preparation for the Marathon when my heart rate would go up to 175. Sheer grit, faith and determination, and an amazing support network led Team McManus to the finish line of the 113th Boston Marathon. Signing off blog posts with see you at the finish line, and all of my energies and focus leading up to Marathon Monday now seem surreal with the Marathon behind me.

The going never got tough during the Marathon. I felt the love, prayers and support from many many friends, and people who I knew on line but never met face to face. I knew once I made it to the starting line, I was going to finish. I knew I was running for those who couldn't or were told they shouldn't run. I ran for polio and post-polio patients everywhere and....I knew I was running for me. I knew my year of hard work was now coming to fruition. I had one mission: to reach the finish line in under 8 hours so there would be someone there to take the timing chip off of my shoe and give me my medal signifying that I had run the 113th Boston Marathon.

The alarm went off at 5 am. Weird dreams and waking up at 1, 3 and finally at 5 did not distress me because I had slept so well on Saturday night.

As we were told at our pre-race pasta dinner on Saturday night, "It's the night before the night before night's sleep that is most important. On Sunday, just stay horizontal."

Our pre-race pasta dinner was a carbo loading buffet feast catered by a local Italian restaurant. Family members and close friends of the Team gathered in the same conference room where we had gathered seven months earlier to meet one another and officially kick off the Race for Rehab Team. Ernst van Dyk, who has since won a record 10 wheelchair titles in the Boston Marathon addressed our Team.

"A life does not end with a disability. It is only a new beginning."

There was a magnificent "Race for Rehab" cake. I did not want to put all that sugar in my system two days before race day. We took our cake home to savor and celebrate after we crossed the finish line.

Team McManus was in perfect rhythm making oatmeal and coffee, getting toast and water, putting the chips on our shoes with no arguments about me wanting to leave too early. There were hugs in the lobby of Spaulding and the mixture of excitement and nervousness. On the bus ride to Hopkinton, I listened to Bernie Siegel's Meditation. I closed my eyes to hear his voice preparing for the day. I did not want to see how long we were traveling to get to Hopkinton. We all joked how the only way back was on our two little feet. Spirits were high on the bus ride out and after finishing my meditation, we chatted about just anything we could think of other than what we all were about to do.

Spaulding's team shared the tent with Mass General Hospital's team. It was a heated tent with pre-race refreshments. We took team pictures and at 8:30

walked to the start with Ashley Bronson, our Events Coordinator. The sun peeked out from behind the clouds and warmed the cool morning air. I drank in the entire scene in awe to realize, I was at the starting line of the 113th Boston Marathon.

We were not going over the timing mats.

I had a wonderful focus for my anxiety. "How would people track us if our chips did not go off and most importantly, how would they know our time?"

Those thoughts were quickly dismissed as we received the oral command from Race Director, Dave McGillivray: "Runners take your marks, get set, go....."

The first several miles felt like any other training run. Because of our early start, the crowds were sparse through Hopkinton and Ashland. I was focused. I knew every step took me one step closer to the finish line. Once we got to the Natick Reservoir, the crowds lined the route and we entered familiar territory. My anxiety subsided as we got into a rhythm of the run. As everyone said, the energy of the crowds carried us along. The scream tunnel of the Wellesley College girls was everything anyone who ever ran Boston told us it would be.

Somewhere around Wellesley, Derv found us among the thousands and thousands of runners. He gave me a huge hug and even ran a little of the way with us. Members of our Race for Rehab team had also found us and we all wished each other well as we journeyed toward Boston.

The crowds were remarkable. They could see that I was not a fast runner and unlike any other road race we had been in, the crowds seemed to sense that I had a special challenge. They would chant "Go Mary Go Mary"; the benefits of Ashley patiently writing my name on my singlet and down my arm. The weather warmed enough so I could run in my short sleeves and singlet. The generosity of the crowds was overwhelming. Families took their time to have orange slices and bananas at the ready. Some had even put their orange slices in individual baggies so we could carry them with us for later in the race. There were cups of water to supplement the water at the water stops, and as we got closer to Boston, bottles of beer.

Once we were in Wellesley, we knew we had it made even though Heartbreak Hill loomed ahead of us. The motto slow and steady wins the race is so true. We did a four-hour half. Some runners may cringe at a four-hour half but there was a 27 mph head wind and it was chilly. Our goal was to make it to the finish line healthy and happy. Since we had run the route from Wellesley to Boston over and over again, we had an incredible psychological advantage. Domenick made us run up Grossman's Hill during training runs going from Brookline to Wellesley; what a joy to only have to run down the hill and then to know that the sign for Newton was just up ahead.

After turning from Route 16 to Commonwealth Avenue, I looked for my friends, the Reillys in front of the famous fire station. I thought that perhaps with the cold and wind and their two little ones, they needed to go home. Shortly after we turned onto Commonwealth Avenue to begin our ascent through the famed hills, Sharon called me on my cell phone. Everyone on Twitter was frantic because we could not be tracked. As one of my dear friends, Nicole Shuman said, God works in creative ways. Sharon got on Twitter and messaged my friend Nicole to let her know we were almost at mile 20 and going strong.

At mile 20, we saw Domenick just as he had promised us. He had tears in his eyes as he embraced Team McManus.

He put his hands on my shoulders and said, "You're gonna qualify - go finish. I'm so proud of you."

In 2009 if you ran the Boston Marathon in under 8 hours as a mobility impaired runner, you qualified to run Boston again.

My cell phone rang. It was Janine checking in with us. As I saw her in the distance standing atop one of the inclines on Heartbreak Hill with her Spaulding Rehab t-shirt and a white long sleeve shirt underneath, I saw an angel who was going to take us to the finish line.

"I'm amazed at how great you guys look," she said.

"We went out slowly and ran steady so we could finish. But I'm sorry about the pace...."

She cut me off and said, "Did you know that the guy who won last year had to be taken off the course? You need to leave those thoughts and all of your baggage out on the roads. Just look at how great you are doing!"

At Cleveland Circle, my son, and Johannes Hirnes, a BU photojournalism grad student were patiently waiting for us to come down Chestnut Hill Avenue. Johannes was given the assignment to capture someone's Boston Marathon journey. He inquired at Brookline Marathon Sports if they knew of anyone who would make a good story and they told him about us. He followed us on our last training run and throughout the day on Marathon Monday.

As we crossed to the Dunkin' Donuts on Beacon Street, our neighbors were waiting with a sign to cheer us on to the finish.

Speaking of signs ....

Bernie Siegel, MD, one of the pioneers in mind/body medicine, and a dear friend since the 1980's, sent me an email telling me to look for the penny. It would be from him and God telling me everything was all right. I found a penny in Wellesley. I told Janine this story as we were walking from the finish line back to the Mandarin Oriental Hotel. At just that moment she looked down and there was another penny. I added it to the 27 cents and the six cents that I carried with me in the back pocket of my capris.

The air was getting cold and raw as we approached Kenmore Square but the crowds were heating up. We knew the finish line was in sight. When we came up out of the underpass there was Hereford Street. Right on Hereford Street and left on Boylston Street. I began to sob seeing the lights of the finish line in the distance. I ran down Boylston Street with all of my might.

Janine refused to cross the finish line with us and took her place on the side saying, "This is all yours."

Even though the chips could not be tracked, the BAA had all of our splits starting with the 5K. We went over to have our chips removed and receive the prize for which we had worked so hard. The pewter medal with a blue and yellow ribbon signifying that we ran 26.2 miles from Hopkinton to Boston on April 20, 2009.

On Mental Toughness

While I focused on the emotional pain I needed to conquer to leave the past behind and become my authentic self to heal mind, body and soul, I did not allow myself to focus on the pain I experienced in my body.

As Janine and I walked back to the Mandarin Oriental Hotel with Autumn, Ruth Anne and Tom walking in front of us, she asked, "How are you feeling physically? Where are you hurting?"

She knew that emotionally I was overcome with joy and exhilaration.

I described the physical pain, and I 'confessed' to her that I had not told her a lot of what I was experiencing during training. She told me there was no need for a confession. She knew I experienced a lot more pain than what I had shared.

There were days when I could not lift one leg or the other because of pain. There were days when my knees would crack and lock. There were days when I could not turn over in bed because of the pain from training. On our 20 mile run in the 14-degree wind chill, I sustained a blister on the heel of my foot which was excruciating for the last four miles of our training run. I knew in my gut that I had not sustained any injuries which would interfere with my crossing that finish line. I deliberately avoided seeking medical intervention as the pains would pass. As different parts of my body experienced pain at different times, I knew this was the painful process of rebuilding muscle and nerve which had been damaged by polio and trauma. I gave Janine an inkling about what I was experiencing and she made suggestions for new stretches, and focused on tweaking nutrition and hydration. We did have to relinquish strength training as we added on miles. It was a delicate balance to listen to what my body was saying but going beyond my limits in order to go the distance of the Boston Marathon. Do you know the most amazing part in all of this? No matter how much pain I experienced, something truly magical happened when it was time to get out and run. I could do it. I did not miss one training session for the entire year due to sickness, injury or pain; a true miracle and a testament to the power of mental toughness.

Hey Hey Look Who's Running!

"The person who finishes the marathon is not the same person who starts the marathon." ~Anonymous

"Finishing a marathon is a state of mind that says anything is possible." ~Anonymous

"Being an athlete is a state of mind which is not bound by age, performance or place in the running pack." ~Jeff Galloway

I tried to resume personal training with Janine after my triumphant 2009 Boston Marathon but was experiencing pain and weakness that interfered with our work. We took a break from working together while I followed up with Western Medicine.

I walked into Spaulding Rehab's Framingham Clinic for a clinic for Prevention Injury for Runners in September of 2009. The treadmills whirred with runners being evaluated by physical therapists. I made eye contact with Kerri who was my first physical therapist at the International Rehab Center for Polio. She smiled and nodded. I waited in line to see Dr. Rosenberg.

As I sat down in the chair he was using to evaluate runners - yes runners - he asked me how I was doing. "Is anything injured? Do you need to come back and see me?"

"Overall I'm doing great. I'm experiencing cervical spine and scapula pain."

"That's very common among polio survivors. I can prescribe a lidocaine patch for you and I'd be happy to see you again in clinic."

"Thank you but I'd prefer to go back to see Dr. El Abd. Thank you for everything. It was great to see you today."

"Before you give me my injection," I said to Dr. El Abd while I sat in my johnny waiting to go into the treatment room, "may I ask you what I need to heal? You know how I use visualization for self-healing and I don't want to have any more injections. I just need a visual."

"Of course," he said exuding warmth and compassion. "Let me first congratulate you on your amazing Boston Marathon run. I know why you had to do it."

He brought in the model of the cervical spine. I listened intently as he explained to me that there was a disc pressing on a nerve at C6 and bone spurs that were causing pain and neurological symptoms in my face, my jaw, and radiating down my arm.

"This is what you need to heal," he said as he pointed to the area on his model.

He wheeled me into the treatment room at Newton Wellesley Hospital where he now practiced, gave me the injection and said he would see me for follow up in two weeks.

"I'm doing well," I told him at my two week follow up visit.

"Let's get you set up with physical therapy again. I have a wonderful therapist that I work with here and she can help you to recover from the marathon."

Catherine Barry was an Australian woman with a no nonsense attitude approach to physical therapy and rehabilitation. She said we needed to correct my alignment and build up core strength.

"I'd like to recommend that you take a break from running for awhile."

I wasn't happy about having to take a break from the sport I now loved but knew I had work to do to get me back on the roads.

She prescribed a cervical traction machine, a pilates ball for core work, and exercises for upper body strength training. After she discharged me from her care, I feverishly worked with the regimen she prescribed eager to get back to my newfound passion of running.

By June of 2010 I was ready to get back on the roads. My comeback race was the Charles River Run 5K. The race director was Paulie. I knew it was fine to be a back of the pack runner in his race. Tom paced me while we enjoyed a scenic course around the Charles River. We held our hands high in triumphant victory after we crossed the finish line. With every mile I ran I defied the diagnosis of Post-Polio Syndrome and moved forward in joy and health in my life.

The blessing of running a race in the back of the pack is you get to share stories and meet amazing people. At the starting line of the inaugural Harvard Pilgrim 10K race, we met a woman just three months out from knee surgery. Her doctor gave her the okay to run/walk the race. A woman asked if this was our first race. She said it was hers and she was concerned that people would wonder why this overweight woman was even in the race. I gave her a short version of my story and a lot of love and support.

"Well then, I'd like to share with you that I am a 15 year breast cancer survivor."

We high fived each other and said, "See you at the finish line."

Tom and I learned from the Charles River Run 5K race to warm up and go out slow especially with the heat. Today was all about finding a comfortable pace and having FUN! We walked through every water station and made sure we hydrated. I had my trusty gel with me and at one hour, we took a 'hit' to keep our muscles fueled. What a thrill to run on the Fourth of July. One family had patriotic music playing on their porch. One woman created a sprinkler with her hose and we ran under it. Spectators stood on front porches and waved flags as we all celebrated freedom.

A father, mother and their daughter took turns pushing their son/brother in a wheelchair. He had a birth defect which resulted in multiple physical challenges. They ran and then walked. They would drop behind us and then go in front of us.

When we caught up with them they said, "Oh no, we gotta speed up."

We passed them and were going to slow down to let them pass us again but they slowed their pace. Tom suggested we push on.

We met a woman who said, "I'm 60 years old and I'm not gonna push myself today in this heat. It's my first 10K."

As she sent her daughter on her way to the finish, she told us that her daughter had lost 100 pounds and discovered the joy of running. She had an article written about her in Redbook; her mom told us how proud she was of her daughter who inspired her to lose over 40 pounds and take up running.

As we came out of the tunnel to sprint the final yards of the 10K, I drank in the joy of the moment. We approached the 50-yard line, and flashed a huge smile. I stood on the field of Gillette Stadium seeing myself on the Jumbotron where world champions play football; where world class entertainers perform.

I turned to Tom and said, "Wait a minute. I want to savor this moment and wave to my adoring fans."

There were fans in the stands cheering runners into the finish line.

July 4th is all about independence, freedom and choosing one's own path.

Everyone has a story. The people I met today chose to not allow circumstances to limit them. Let freedom ring!

Training for the Tufts 10K   **September 26, 2010**

Standing at the finish line of the 2009 Tufts 10K, the announcer called out the names of the finishers.

In between runners she said, "Are you going to let anyone ever tell you you can't do something?!"

God's voice rang out loud and clear. I didn't know if I would ever be able to return to running after crossing the finish line of the 2009 Boston Marathon. I lacked flexibility and strength in my cervical spine. There was a lot of pain including radiating arm pain. Catherine had me return to the theraband exercises once prescribed by Allison. I could barely pull the 'green' band to 'row a boat' or to pull down over the door jamb. I could barely do the exercises on the pilates ball without weights. I could not do a calf leg raise on my left leg. We eliminated weights over 3 pounds for upper body strength training and eliminated all weights with lower body strength training. I maintained at 15 squats and alternated with different exercises using gravity and increasing 'hold' time to 'stress' the muscles to build strength.

Hearing those words "Are you going to ever let anyone tell you you can't do something" and seeing women of all shapes, sizes, abilities and paces crossing the finish line, I made a vow with myself that I would be back to run the 2010 Tufts 10K for Women. It took 9 months of intensive training to get back on the roads.

When I joined Twitter in December of 2008, Kevin Green invited me to join his on line running community, "Just Finish." His philosophy was to call all walkers, runners, cyclists of every athletic ability to just finish whatever goals people set for themselves. I found incredible support with this community while I trained for the 2009 Boston Marathon and on line friends, like Derv, turned into real life friends. It was a bold move for me to invite someone to run with me; it meant releasing the years of taunting and teasing, and embracing the joy of running and guiding another woman runner. I was inspired to invite Deborah, Derv's wife, to run the Tufts 10K with me.

Deborah had never run over 4 miles. It was my turn to inspire and encourage her as others had done for me when I began my running career. Deborah is a beautiful woman inside and out and today we had our 5 mile training run. She knew if she could run 5 miles, she could run the Tufts 10K. There was a magical rhythm to our pacing and non-stop conversation as we bonded during our run. The time literally flew by. Our goal was to make sure Deborah knew she could run for 5 miles without being concerned about the pace. After our run, Tom had a scrumptious brunch waiting for us.

There was ease, joy and laughter as we feasted on the food that Tom lovingly prepared; omelettes, toast, juice and coffee. Derv however, was not happy that Tom set the expectations for what a post-run meal is supposed to be.

"My wife thought pop tarts and cereal was a great meal to have waiting for her after a run before you cooked this omelette. Now I'll have to cook eggs benedict to compete."

In between mouthfuls, Derv suggested that we need to have a Team name.

"How about Sparkling Divas?"

We loved it! We may not have the perfect runners' bodies but, through running, Deborah and I let our spirits shine.

Love, laughter, a great run and good food made for a wonderful recipe for confidence as we prepared to toe the starting line of the 2010 Tufts 10K.

"There is no better way to feel self-confidence than by instilling confidence in another." ~Mary McManus

Running the 2010 Tufts 10K as the Sparkling Divas is a day I shall always remember and cherish. Deborah's goal was to run a 5 mile Turkey Trot on Thanksgiving Day. When I asked her about running Tufts with me, she decided it would give her the motivation she needed to train for her initial goal.

Race day gave us a bright and beautiful October morning after a week in which we had four straight days of rain. I decided to layer because I knew if the sun came out while crossing the Massachusetts Avenue Bridge, it would be brutally hot. I changed from shorts to capris because I did not want my knee joints to feel cold prior to the race. Derv and Deborah, and their adorable son Alex arrived at 9:30 sharp. The nervous energy of the Sparkling Divas was palpable as we got our water, went to the bathroom, decided what we would need to bring, what we could leave at our house, took photos and piled into our car to park and take the T to the Boston Common. We had plenty of time before the race to check out the Expo. We did our warm up with the herd of runners led by an energetic instructor, and had one last pit stop before heading to the starting line. Deborah acknowledged she felt a little overwhelmed by it all. I told her to think of this as just another training run or as my fellow runners like to say - taking our victory lap. We gave hugs and high fives to our wonderful support crew of Tom, Derv and Alex, and each other, and were pumped up as we made our way to the starting line. I realized during our warm up that I had not put on my watch and my heart monitor. Subconsciously I knew I wasn't supposed to focus on time or heart rate.

I had no idea how many minutes it took us to cross the starting line. For the first time in a race, I let go of time. I let go of all the fears and angst of being last, of having to catch up, of being less than the rest of the runners and all the voices I internalized and harbored for so many years. I was not going to let the myths and untruths about me rob me of enjoying this incredible moment running side by side with a dear friend. What beautiful moments flowed out on the course. We talked about nothing and everything. As I instilled confidence in Deborah about the run (having run Tufts in 2008 and having trained along the route with Tom just a week ago), I felt my own confidence soar. It was a mid-day race which can be challenging for fueling and pacing. I spaced out my breakfast over an hour and had a banana pre-race. I lived in the flow and went with the flow of the moment.

When we got to mile 1 the clock read 24:00 minutes.

"What we did a 24 minute/mile pace" was a brief thought that flashed through my mind. I knew that wasn't right and so what if it had been? I decided to see the time of our next mile and then would know what pace we were doing and how long it took to cross the starting line. I know I know I wasn't going to focus on time this time but old habits die hard!

As it turns out we did a 15 minute/mile pace for the first mile and a 16:00 minute/mile pace for mile 2. A great pace for the start of the race. I saw that we were holding a 16 minute/mile pace for miles 3 and 4. After that I let go of looking at the time. My goal was to enjoy providing support to Deborah, a friendship forged through the amazing sport of running, who was about to accomplish something she had never done before. My role was to help her push past any thoughts of limitation. Our strategy was to run the entire race (a first for Deborah) but walk through the water stations. As we made the turn at the BU bridge heading back into Boston and Deborah saw the Massachusetts Avenue bridge in the distance she said, "We have to run all the way over that?"

I smiled. I told her stories of our marathon training runs with our meltdowns and hysterical moments. Who would have ever dreamed that I was doing for my friend what so many runners had done for me. I was talking her through a run, keeping her distracted as we ticked off the miles and instilled confidence in her health and fitness journey.

When we got to mile 4, Deborah said it was a psychological milestone. She knew we were more than halfway there. As we approached the bridge, I suggested that she relax and enjoy the beautiful view. She stopped to take a photo. Once we got to Commonwealth Avenue, Deborah kicked it into high gear - and I mean high gear. Talk about a negative split.

"Are you okay?" she asked me.

"Oh yeah. Let's just get to our guys at the finish line!"

At the last water stop, there were men in tuxedoes holding the water cups on a cardboard box as waiters hold a tray.

What a fantastic touch Tufts 10K!

We began passing runners and walkers. I excitingly said, "Look where we are Deborah! All we have to do is to run a little farther to get to the chute down the finish line."

"Really? We're almost there?"

"Yes indeed. We are almost there!"

I had to kick it into high gear. Deborah was now setting the pace for us.

We turned the corner toward the finish line.

Emotions welled up within me as I realized the overwhelming meaning of the moment for Deborah and for me. I told her to drink in every minute of coming down the chute to the finish line.

As we approached the finisher's chute, we heard "And here come the Sparkling Divas. Mary McManus and Deborah Woodbury Doiron. Go Sparkling Divas. You're almost there. Great job."

After we crossed the finish line Tom told me he was by the announcer and asked her to announce our arrival. We saw Tom, Derv, and Alex with Alex holding a sign he made that said, "Go Sparkling Divas!"

When Deborah and I crossed the finish line, we hugged each other tightly and cried. We did indeed start strong and finish stronger, the motto of the Tufts 10K for Women. What a thrilling moment to share in the incredible joy and celebrate my friend's first 10K race. What a difference a year made for me as one year ago I wasn't even sure I would be able to return to the sport I had come to love.

Christmas Magic at the Jingle Bell 5K   December 20, 2010

What to my wondering eyes should appear at the starting line of the Jingle Bell 5K, another Paulie race, but my teammates from the 2009 Spaulding Race for Rehab Team. With almost 5,000 runners what were the chances that we would bump into Suzanne and Sarah. Christmas magic was definitely in the air.

Tom and I took our place among the runners. I told him to kick my behind to the finish. Christmas music blared through Davis Square and at 11:04 we were off. Despite the cold air, I was intently focused on my goal for the race. I knew in my heart I was going to set a PR. We got to mile 1 and I looked at my watch. 13:21.

"Tom what do you have for our time?"

"Oh this has to be wrong; I have like a 13 minute/mile pace."

"No that's about right."

The 2nd mile had rolling hills and I only had to take one walking break after my heart rate climbed over 171. It was a fast course.

Mile 2 to the finish seemed like an eternity to me.

Although I knew I was on pace for a PR because our time at mile 2 was 27:21 - a 14 minute/mile pace, when the officials told us we had only about a half mile to go, I had this perception that I was not going to hit my PR.

I saw my watch hit 42:00 and I heard this voice say "Don't worry if you don't do it. It's okay."

The next thing I knew I was crossing the finish line and saw my watch at 42:50.

So how did I take one minute and 23 seconds off of a race from two months ago? What is happening to allow this body to transform from finishing last to being able to run at a 13:38 minute pace? I have to thank my running and life partner Tom. He coached, coaxed, cajoled and talked me through the race, telling me what an inspiration I am. He really kicked my behind when he wouldn't let me stop at the water stop. He told me we had our own and it was a lot better for me than what they had at the water stop. He did not want me to slow down my pace and I am so glad he did that for me. He kept me in the zone telling me to listen to the music and breathe with the music. He told me after the run these are the tricks he uses when he is on a long run especially in the cold weather which can tend to take one's breath away. I am so grateful to him for sharing in my healing journey. My average heart rate was 167 with a peak of 185. That's not too shabby for this girl who is going to be 57 in five days.

A Return to Camp Hyannis

February 28, 2011

I was unable to run during Hyannis Marathon, Half Marathon and 10K Weekend in 2010 while recovering from my phenomenal Boston Marathon run. While I was sidelined from running, I was able to participate in the weekend. Paulie generously donated a table to me at the Expo. I had books of inspirational poetry to sell, and a story to inspire the runners. Frank Shorter and Bill Rodgers signed my Boston Marathon bib.

Frank wrote, "You're unbelievable."

Bill signed his name and dated it 2010.

On Friday, as I was packing to go to Hyannis Marathon Weekend, I felt the presence of Joe Stetz and of all those wonderful memories of Badger Day Camp. We get to see old friends who we only see once a year at Hyannis i.e. returning campers, meet up with friends who are going for the first time, and make new friends. I felt Joe's presence as I was going into the weekend and knew he was going to be with me when I ran the race. Why was I so anxious about Hyannis? It's in the middle of a New England winter. While nobody likes to run in the cold, it is a particular challenge for me. This winter has been grueling but I knew I had done everything I could to train for the race. Deborah and I were running together again. She invited one of her friends to join the Sparkling Divas. I was anxious running with someone who I would meet for the first time at the starting line.

After checking into our room, we unpacked and laid out everything we would need for race day. It was time to head out to the Expo. Frank Shorter and Bill Rodgers would not be returning campers ahem speakers this year. We reunited with Dick Hoyt and Kathy Boyer of Team Hoyt. Dick recently had knee surgery and would not be running. I felt nostalgic about our reunion with Dick and purchased an autographed copy of his book, "Devoted". The guest speakers for the pre-race pasta dinner were Jack Fultz, 1976 Boston Marathon winner in the "run for the hoses" race, and Jimmy Garcia, an ultra marathoner and winner of the 2003 Hyannis Marathon. We waited in line for an autographed poster of Jack Fultz. I shared my inspirational journey with him. Running greats resonate to the joy of the challenges I have overcome.

I texted Sparkling Diva Deborah. We met up at the Expo psyching ourselves up for the next day's run.

Campers arrived with coolers and running clothes in tow. The energy was electric.

We bumped into returning campers exchanging hugs with "How was your year?"

Tom and I went for a swim to stay loose. We showered, changed and headed to the mess hall - I mean ballroom for the pre-race pasta dinner. Here's where the camp theme really kicks into high gear. The food is lousy but you don't care. It's overcooked pasta, wilted salad from marinating in salad dressing for too long and focaccia bread. Instead of singing 99 bottles of beer on the wall, there are 99 bottles of beer (or more) stocked in the bar which runners imbibe to add to the carbo loading. We sat with Mike with whom we have shared previous years' pre-race pasta dinners getting caught up on each other's lives. We shared photos in our phones of the family and were joined by two new campers who were friends of Mike. I called fellow camper Ric to see where he was and he was on his way with a host of campers old and new. He asked if I would save him a table - honest to God - just like we used to do at camp only we'd throw a sweatshirt or use our hand to save a seat for our fellow camper. I turned the chairs in at the banquet table for them to reserve their seats.

I met Jimmy Garcia and viewed all of his belt buckle bling from his ultramarathon runs. We hung out for awhile before saying good night knowing tomorrow was race day. Ric introduced me to Mark and Laura. Laura is a Boston Children's Hospital miracle treated for scoliosis. Tom was running the 2011 Boston Marathon to raise money for Children's Hospital. She may have two rods in her back, but she is going to run her first Marathon in May. We inspired each other with our running journeys.

I had the usual pre-race anxiety dreams including one in which my alarm didn't go off. I awoke before the alarm and slowly stretched and calmed my nerves. We awoke to snow; about 2 inches on the golf course outside of our window and flakes steadily coming down. We brought our pre-race breakfast adding to it from the Starbucks in the lobby.

No matter what I was going to run this race today. I calmed the butterflies in my stomach by listening to my iPod running playlist, meditating on the falling snow, recalling the words of Joe Stetz and drinking in all of the love and prayers from Twitter and Facebook that had been sent to me. Tom listened to his mP3 meditations.

9:00 am:

Time to meet up with my Sparkling Diva teammates and check in with fellow campers. The Expo space was overflowing with campers ahem runners standing shoulder to shoulder to keep warm before gun time. I could feel my nerves go into high gear when we started to walk outside to "warm up." Out of over 5,000 runners, we bumped into Chris Russell before we made our way outside. Chris interviewed me for his RunRunLive podcast. He was going to try to run after a calf injury but knew it wasn't meant to be. In true runner style, since he couldn't run, he would cheer on and support the runners. He gave us trash bags to keep us warm and dry and suggested we wait to head out to the start.

10:00 am Gun Time:

We heard the Star Spangled Banner from the back of the pack and saw everyone begin to move forward. Usually at the start of a race I feel my heart pound. I have a difficult time getting into a rhythm, but not today. I was swept up in the moment of the snowflakes dancing, the joy of being a part of a wonderful running community and all the magic that is Camp Hyannis. Amy, Deborah and I ran and talked with ease. The beauty of the sport of running is that total strangers can become instant friends; just add a pair of running shoes and the pavement.

At mile 3, I checked my watch. 43:00 minutes.

When I smiled Deborah smiled and asked, "What are you grinning at over there?"

"We just did a 14 minute/mile pace."

We didn't look ahead of us or behind us and stayed in the moment. My breathing was even and my body felt strong despite the elements of a mix of snow and rain. There was mercifully no wind to contend with even as we ran by the beach. I told Deborah and Amy about my Camp Hyannis theme; I teased myself and said I am the camper everyone hates for having so much camp spirit. We all laughed as we ran dancing with the snowflakes. I noticed the beautiful scenery and experienced the expanse of ocean and sky. I felt euphoric that I was back out on the road in Hyannis. I was wet and cold and my feet were soaked but none of that mattered. I had one thought in my mind - to cross that finish line.

Tom was out on the course running his half marathon as a training run for his 2011 Boston Marathon run. I would occasionally send angels to bless his calf. He had a torn gastroc muscle several weeks before Hyannis. His physical therapist gave him the green light to run Hyannis but told him to take it easy. I asked the angels to keep him running safe, strong and at a steady pace.

After mile 5, we picked up the pace but wanted to leave enough in the tank for a strong finish. The volunteers were wonderful cheering us on telling us girls we were doing a great job.

"You're almost there," they shouted!

We took off into a sprint; Deborah and Amy surged ahead of me and I couldn't keep up but what a blessing that I did not feel left behind as I once did with a polio limp. My joints were tight and I knew that I had done so much better than what we ran at the Tufts 10K. I wanted to head into the finish line uninjured and without getting sick. I crossed the finish line at 1:30, taking 6 minutes off of my 2010 Tufts 10K. Chris Russell was there as I finished and he took my hand in a cross between a high five and a hand shake.

Boy did that feel good!

Deborah, Amy and I hugged. We were all Sparkling Divas!

At the finish line, while waiting for Tom, I met one of my younger runner friend's mom. I could see that the apple didn't fall from the tree. Ashley's mom overflowed with love and warmth. We talked about where Ashley was on the course. I had no idea where Tom might be since he left his phone in the room. I told Ashley's mom how much Ashley inspired me with her health and fitness journey. Her mom beamed with pride and told me how Ashley shared my journey with her. We chatted about the great sport of running and hugged as I left her waiting to cheer on her daughter at the finish.

Tom would soon be crossing the finish line and would need the tub for an ice bath. I needed a hot shower. While walking through the Expo hallway, I bumped into my fellow campers. We shared our race stories, and high fived each other for making it through tough weather conditions.

After Tom came in with a great performance; a 2:22 half post injury, he took his ice bath. Camp Race T-shirts, bling and memories were all packed! We hung out in the hallways savoring the final moments of Camp Hyannis, and exchanging race stories. It was a very Kumbaya kind of moment. Coolers were empty and laundry bags were filled with dirty running clothes. Instead of everyone signing the autograph book on the last day of camp and giving each other our addresses, we looked for each other on Facebook to become friends.

Today I am sore and tired. I am proud of my running ability, but even more grateful to know I can trust my body. I can continue to train and grow stronger and healthier with each passing year.

Is it hard work? Oh yeah! Is it worth it? Oh yeah! Do I get to have a happy childhood at the age of 57? Oh yeah.

March and April of 2011 were dedicated to fund raising and supporting Tom's Boston Marathon run. My nephew died by suicide on March 4. I was grateful to be able to have the opportunity to immerse myself in the marathon activities while maintaining my health and wellness in the wake of this tragedy.

Hey Hey Look Who's Running   June 5, 2011

Three years later ... the first Sunday in June ... The Corrib Pub Run 5K. My first road race ever in 2008 on my road to the Boston Marathon.

Today's weather - glorious. My kind of weather - sunny and a cool breeze. I meditated, breathed and stretched and mentally prepared myself for another road race. During my meditation I pondered, why do I run? Why do I run road races? Initially I ran because I had something to prove. Then I ran because I had something to prove and focused on PR's. Now I run because I have nothing to prove but I enjoy running road races. I love the energy, the camaraderie and the joy of being physically active feeling good inside my body.

As Tom and I walked down the stairs to the field, we reflected on these past several years.

"You do realize," he said, "that if you did not take exquisite care of yourself and dedicate yourself to your journey, you'd be in a wheelchair."

I paused on the stairs as my breath caught. My eyes welled with tears. My heart opened overflowing with gratitude keenly aware of how blessed I am to have created this miracle of healing in my life.

What a thrill to return to the race that was my first road race. How I love being able to run side by side with Tom as he encourages and supports me and we find that delicate balance between challenging me but not pushing too hard crossing into the land of suffering. We bumped into one of his colleagues from Childrens Hospital and had a great pre-race conversation. Just as I was thinking I should have brought a piece of fruit with me, orange slices seemed to appear out of nowhere. Perfect!

The first mile had an uphill and we were running hard. Tom reminded me that we need to keep a lot in the tank for the hills at the end as well. We were a part of the sea of 2000 runners through the first mile. Emotions welled up within me as I ran with the pack.

I heard Spirit speak to me and say, "There is no disconnection unless you create it."

We made it to mile marker 1 and the volunteer told us our time was 16 minutes gun time. Tom and I looked at our times and it was 15:00. At first I felt frustrated because I thought we were running faster than the time reflected. I told myself to release all of that; allow myself to tune into my body and enjoy the moments of being out on the road. When I let go of all that doesn't matter, I allow myself to experience the incredible joy of running in a road race. I love the energy of the cheers and the energy of the runners. I was passed and I passed walkers. There was no competition. I am setting the pace and running my own race. I have said those words so many times. Today I felt those words deep in my heart and soul. When I strip away what doesn't matter, I can let in all that joy!

The neighborhoods came out to cheer and set up their own water stops in addition to the water stops set up by the race organizers. They had hoses. Even though it wasn't a broiling hot day, running through a sprinkler is refreshing and FUN! Now it may not seem like a big deal to you to run through a sprinkler but it sure is to me. I am blessed to have had the challenges of polio and trauma. I take great pleasure in the little things in life. I am so grateful. I can deeply appreciate the joy of running free on a summer's day. I lived through the summer of 1971 when I was a prisoner in my own home. We couldn't go out after 5 pm because my father came to the house in alcoholic rages. I feel deeply grateful and appreciate the gift of the moments of movement after paralysis, so many surgeries, a leg brace, a cast and having felt trapped in this body for decades.

Tom said, "Look we are at mile 2"

"Where?"

"Right up there".

"Hey Hey look who's running," we heard.

It was John McDermott, also known as Mac, the President of our L Street Running Club volunteering for the race. He high fived us and smiled. He radiated love for us. He came running after us to give us our time.

"31 minutes."

"That's gun time," I playfully shouted to Mac over my shoulder.

I knew we had taken a minute off of our second mile and smiled but I smiled even more deeply to feel a part of this amazing running community. I knew we had only 1.1 miles left. I was leaving nothing on the road. I felt well and we picked up the pace until...oh no I forgot about this hill. I decided to walk briskly to bring down my heart rate a little and leave some in the tank for a strong finish.

We turned the corner to the long downhill to the finish line. Tom told me to lean forward and take small steps.

"Let gravity do the work."

As we approached the finish Tom said to me, "This is it! Go for it."

I channeled Forrest Gump, feeling glorious sprinting to the finish line. I didn't care about the time. I cared about the movement and being in the moment. I cared about opening up my body to full throttle. I loved hearing the cheering of the crowds as I took off. I ran the race in 44:39 taking a minute off of my time from 2009. Despite the time on the clock that wasn't an overall PR, I had the best time. Thanks to the hills, my average heart rate was 160 with a peak of 176. The peak of my target zone for my age is 140.

Yeah hey hey - look who's running now!

After my nephew's death by suicide in March, the pain in my heart manifested in my body. I felt as though I couldn't run anymore after the Corrib Pub race in June. I turned away from the running community at a time when I most needed their love and support. My health and fitness regimen and the fire in my belly was extinguished when he jumped into the icy waters of the Atlantic Ocean. I practiced yoga 5-6 days a week seeking, and searching for inner peace. I was, as the song says, looking for love in all the wrong places.

I slowly emerged from my fog of grief and, in April 2013 decided it was time to reconnect with my Race for Rehab teammates. Every year we received an invitation to return to the Mandarin Oriental Hotel to celebrate with the new team of Race for Rehab runners. On April 15, 2013, Tom and I walked up the steps to the Spaulding Rehab reception. Unlike 2009, we were able to walk up the steps with ease. I remembered the triumphant moments of being greeted by teammates and staff from Spaulding along with my friends who gathered to welcome back the conquering hero. David Storto, the President of Spaulding Rehab asked me to give a speech. Standing with my BAA foil wrapped around me and my medal adorning my neck, he said that I was a shining example of what Spaulding Rehab was all about. It was an Oscar worthy moment in which I expressed my gratitude to Spaulding, to my therapists, to my friends gathered in the ballroom for their emotional and financial support. We raised $10,535 for Spaulding.

Emotions welled up within me while we watched runners coming down Boylston Street heading to the finish line through the floor to ceiling glass windows.

After I gave my speech, we were whisked away to a beautiful suite upstairs at the Mandarin. The physical therapists from Spaulding were waiting for us. As soon as I got on the table, my legs cramped and my whole body shivered. As two physical therapists worked to help me warm up, one of them took off my running shoes and gasped. I was terrified for a moment wondering what they saw. They said they had never seen a blood blister that big in their lives. They massaged my legs, wrapped me in warm, soft blankets and asked me if there was anything else I needed. One of the women from the Development Office ordered food for us. Since we had taken almost eight hours to finish our run, the food had run out at the reception.

"Could you hear us banging on the windows as you came down Boylston Street?" Ashley Bronson asked as the other members of the Development Team chimed in.

We filled our plates with an array of foods from the buffet table, bid on silent auction items and made our way into the 3rd room of the suite. We had an emotional reunion with our former teammates and their families.

"I was very emotional during WBZ's coverage of the early start this morning," I told one of our teammates.

"You inspired me more than you'll ever know," he replied.

We both paused side by side as if in trance remembering our 2009 Boston Marathon run in front of the windows watching the runners coming down Boylston Street.

The excitement was building as Spaulding runners being tracked by the Development Team crossed the finish line and were making their way back to the hotel to be regaled as Team McManus was once regaled. Tom and I were debating whether or not to go downstairs to cheer on our friends. We looked at the clock on the wall and decided that we'd wait until we got the text notification that they hit the 40K mark. The text never came. At 2:49 pm we heard a boom that sounded like a cannon in the distance. It's not a sound we'd associate with Marathon Monday. Everyone paused. Twelve seconds later the hotel shook and white smoke filled the air outside the glass windows. My brave teammate looked outside.

"It's bad. Very bad. It's a tragedy," he said.

The hotel staff, poised and calm, led us out of the hotel. Tom and I walked as quickly as we could the few miles back to our car that we parked near Brookline Village along South Huntington Avenue. With sirens blaring and helicopters flying overhead, SWAT Teams and emergency vehicles raced toward the finish line.

The OneRun   May 25, 2013

The moving pre-race ceremony began including 30 seconds of silence for those who lost their lives in the bombings. There was music, inspirational speeches and not a dry eye in the crowd while 8 year old Martin Richard's church choir sang the National Anthem. Martin made his first communion at the Church and was one of those whose lives was taken on 4/15/13. Tom and I had our arms around each other. Everyone held each other in a spiritual embrace.

Race Director Alain Ferry gave us the signal and we were off crossing the one mile to go mark in Kenmore Square. Four years ago, Team McManus headed toward the finish line with strength, courage and determination. The somber mood was quite a contrast to the celebratory mood we experienced when we ran on April 20, 2009. When we got to Hereford Street, I took a deep breath. I knew we were going back to the Mandarin Oriental Hotel across the street from The Forum where the second bomb exploded. As we passed in front of the Mandarin, we stopped for a brief moment to give our thanks to the staff who ensured our safety. How healing and wonderful to see the two doormen who were there on Marathon Monday and express our gratitude to them, and be back on a part of Boylston Street I was terrified to visit.

I told Tom I was ready to sprint to the finish line. I said a prayer as we ran by The Forum. I sobbed as the crowds cheered. We were surrounded by runners with their bib numbers from Marathon Monday and throngs of people who had been touched by the tragic events of April 15. At the finish line we shared stories. We hugged. We cried. We healed. Despite the cold and the rain, the love and energy of the community kept us warm.

Before the start of the OneRun, Alain said, "You are out there to run for those who can't."

Those words echoed in my ears. I ran the 2009 Boston Marathon for those who couldn't and for those who were told they shouldn't run or would never be able to run again. I was delivering a message of healing, hope and possibility. Today I was one with the survivors knowing the long road they have for healing. I knew that they, like me, would be able to go the distance. Here I was running the last mile with a deep connection to the survivors of the bombing knowing in every fiber of my being what it's like to work to regain mobility and to recover from the trauma of facing death. Emotions roiled within me as we listened to the pre-race ceremony speakers and then as we reclaimed Boylston Street as our own. It was a wake up call for me to get back to the sport and community of running. On June 16, 2013, I rolled up my yoga mat for the last time, got a new pair of kicks at Marathon Sports and began a new training plan joining the community of runners that would henceforth be known as Boston Strong.

In February of 2014 we returned to Camp Hyannis. The mood was somber in the wake of the bombings but the sense of community and camaraderie was stronger than ever. Tom was running the Half Marathon. It was a perfect day for him to get his Half Marathon PR. I saw him flash the eye of the tiger at the start of the race. As the time came and went for when Tom should have crossed the finish line, I was getting more than a little concerned. One of the members of the Race for Rehab team threw her body over the railing that separated the runners from the spectators.

"Tom saved us out there," she said.

My heart skipped a beat.

"What do you mean? What happened?" flashing back to 2:49 on April 15ᵗʰ.

"Karis and I were sitting down at mile 3 crying. We didn't know how we were going to be able to do this. He stopped and talked to us. We got back in the race but had no idea what we were doing. You know this is our first big race. Tom kept an eye on us before taking off again and even though we told him to go run his own race, he stayed with us, pacing us and getting us to the finish line."

A few moments later Tom crossed the finish line with Karis.

We were invited to the Race for Rehab post-race celebration at a restaurant in Hyannis Center. Tom was celebrated as a hero for sacrificing his own race to help newbie runners Karis and Amanda. He helped them to physically run the race and get them mentally prepared to take on Boston.

"I didn't sacrifice anything," Tom said. "It's runner's code. You don't leave someone out there suffering if you can help."

The Gift of Running   May 21, 2014

"I learned that the only requirement to be part of this wonderful group was to run. I didn't have to be fast. I didn't have to be great. I just had to run. And that's when running became not just something that I do but something that is a part of who I am." ~John Bingham

After I wrote the poem "Running the Race," I was intrigued with the line, "while in my mind I focused on winning a 10K race." I felt exhilarated, uplifted, excited, transformed and indeed my curiosity was piqued.

Running? Mary McManus? aka "Easy Out Alper" - um a rather unlikely combination to say the least.

But not impossible despite all appearances to the contrary. It's been a healing odyssey filled with ups and downs, trials and triumphs just like life. I wasn't sure if I was going to make it back to running and a state of health after my nephew's suicide in 2011.

After last year's Boston Marathon, I knew I needed to return to running and the running community.

I started from the beginning building up mileage, running a few 5K's and building strength in the Aquatics Therapy program at Spaulding Rehab.

I set my sights on running the Tufts 10K. I was up to 5 miles again in my distance.

While out on a training run I realized how running is more than the miles. It's more than the time.

I felt something shift inside of me. I felt what a gift it is to run. The gift of running is the ability to live fully in the present moment.

I began to challenge myself; to train in earnest and be fully present. I used strategies every good coach uses. Focus on your breathing. Feel your footsteps. Let's see if you can pick up the pace. Make it to that house up ahead; to that Stop sign. I took in the beauty of the scene and felt a unity, a harmony, a wholeness in the midst of it all. I ended up doing a negative split of .50 seconds between mile 2 and 3 with an average pace of 15:33/mile for that last mile. Somehow on that run and somehow during these past 7 years I came to the realization that running is now a part of who I am. It is a gift and one that I treasure. I feel the gratitude and appreciation flow through me every time I lace up my running shoes and go out for a run. It is a gift that keeps me present feeling fully alive in the moment regardless of the challenges in my life. If the time comes when in my physical form I am no longer able to run, running will always be a part of who I am. All that I have learned and who I have become through running shall forever remain.

One Moment in Time: Race Report Bill Rodgers 5K Run/Walk to Benefit Prostate Cancer   August 10, 2014

I was open to whatever my body was going to be able to do today. My mantra for today's race was light and joy. I wanted to thoroughly enjoy the day. I slept well and didn't have the usual pre-race jitters. I had a good breakfast of a bagel, oatmeal, banana and orange juice. What a luxury to be able to get up at 6:45am on a race day and drive 10 minutes to the start of the race.

I had a sense of trust that this was going to be a good day.

When we arrived, race director Alain Ferry whom you may recall was also the organizer of the OneRun greeted us. He had been following my blog posts about my intention to PR for the race. He gave me a big bear hug and asked me to remind him what my goal was for today's race.

"I hope we see 47:00 minutes or less on the clock when you cross that finish line. Remind me again of your name?" Alain asked extending his hand to Tom.

"It's Tom."

"We met at the Heartbreak Hill Marathon weekend. I remember you."

He warmly shook Tom's hand and said, "Well I've got about a million things to do. See you back here."

I reconnected with Bill Rodgers at his table while he sold copies of his book, "Marathon Man: My 26.2 Mile Journey From Unknown Grad Student to the Top of the Running World." He remembered me and my story from Hyannis.

"How did you like the book?" Bill asked me.

"I loved it Bill," I answered with a big smile. I shared with him parts of the book that resonated with me.

"Life is hard," he said to me. "That's why we run. If we can tough it out on the roads, we know we can tough it out in life."

Bill turned and introduced us to his girlfriend Karen.

"I overheard your conversation with Billy. You've had an amazing journey. I'm a breast cancer survivor and started running in my 40's after the diagnosis."

We instinctively hugged even though we just met each other.

"Let's get everyone over to the starting line," Alain commanded through his bullhorn.

Pre-race announcements talked about the importance of supporting research, early detection and treatment for Prostate Cancer. Alain asked for a show of hands of those running affected by cancer. There was an astounding number of hands raised in the crowd. Alain handed Bill Rodgers the mic. He shared how he is a prostate cancer survivor.

"It is the #2 leading cause of cancer deaths among American men. We need to pay as much attention to prostate cancer for men as we do for breast cancer for women."

Bill Rodgers went on in his pre-race remarks. "Running and walking is a simple little sport but we as Americans can use it to change the world."

And then it was gun time and time for me to write another chapter of my story.

We started at the front of the pack with Bill Rodgers off to our left. I went out running fast through the campus of Boston College. Thirty years ago I received my Masters in Social Work degree and spent many many hours on that beautiful campus. The field took off and I adhered to my race plan. We'd run the downhill and I'd run for as long as I could and then move into race walking. When we got to the rolling hills of Commonwealth Avenue, I race walked. The sun was bright and the day heated up fast. We were grateful there was no humidity and we could go on the sidewalk for shade. We brought frozen water bottles that I used for hydration and to keep cool.

Mile 1 - 14:33 pace. I was blown away by my time but I knew that anything could happen over the next two point one miles.

Tom kept checking in with me. How was I feeling? Did anything hurt? I didn't talk much which is very unusual for me and I was breathing hard. I had a single-minded goal but I was running from the inside out.

In my training runs I had stopped to take a "water break." At times I slowed my pace, but kept moving forward. We stopped for about 30 seconds at the water stop before it was time to tackle the hill with a 221' elevation.

Mile 2 - time was almost 30 minutes.

Okay I think I can. I think I can. I've got this. I can do this.

Tom said to me "What do we do with hills?"

"We eat them for breakfast," I managed to get out.

To the top of Beacon Street and a right onto College Road.

A right onto Commonwealth Avenue heading toward the finish.

Alain came out on his bike, "Oh there you are. "Come on you're almost there."

I was hot and my tank was close to empty.

As we headed toward the finish Alain told me I had less than a minute for my PR.

People gathered to cheer me on.

Alain was just on the other side of the finish line.

I sprinted to the finish and the finish clock read 46:57 gun time!

I knew in my heart and soul that I crossed more than a finish line. As I told Alain, I reclaimed my life. The essence of who I am took center stage. It was another moment of redemption achieved through running. I wrung out the grief from my nephew's death. I ran as Boston Strong rinsing out the trauma of 4/15/13 with sweat and tears.

It's been one hell of a journey back since Charlie Louis Alper tragically and violently died on March 4th of 2011. Thanks to Alain and the OneRun, I knew I had to come back to the sport that had transformed my life. I realized it was more than coming back to running. It was setting a goal and once again challenging myself. It was opening up to see what my body could do leaving nothing on the roads. It was about testing my mettle and letting go of fear.

Alain shared with me that he didn't expect to find us as far up on Commonwealth Avenue as close to the finish line as he did. He was concerned about the heat and was coming to provide support regardless of the time on the clock. When he saw how close we were to the finish, he wanted that PR for me as much as I did. I felt as though I was being pulled into the vortex of the finish line by his loving energy and all those cheering me on.

"I saw you start to cry and then I saw a look come across your face. You dug deep during that sprint," he said to me. "It was quite a moving moment for me as a Race Director to watch you come across that finish line with such visible fierce determination."

During that final sprint, Tom let me set the pace. He could tell I was in the zone. Tom wept with me when we crossed the finish line. We both knew that I left pain, fear and doubt out on the course and in its wake, strength, courage, confidence, and healing surged.

Gratitude filled my heart for Facebook friends who I met for the first time who cheered me on and took photos, and to Alain who was there to celebrate and tend to me post race.

"Here is an ice water for you. Go get in the shade and here's a couple of oranges for you and Tom. I'm so proud of you!"

Today was one moment in time - many moments in time that I will always cherish when I look back on my adventures as runner girl.

A Post-Race Celebration Surprise

When Alain rode up on his bicycle and said, "Oh there you are," Tom and I thought he was just coming out to check on the back of the packers and walkers still out on the course. He came looking for me to cheer me onto the finish. As the runner's fog cleared in my mind from those final minutes of my race, I remembered Alain on his bike riding along in front of us cheering me on.

"Come on Mary. You can do this," and then counting down the time standing on just the other side of the finish line.

It was a deeply personal moment for me yet one that was shared among the runners gathered around the finish. Their energy, love and support drew me to the finish line. There were a few people I knew from Facebook in the crowd but it was mostly a crowd of people that I'd never met, led by Alain. They were inspired by my fierce determination to bring home a strong finish.

As we hydrated and enjoyed a post race orange with sticky hands...

"Hi Mary. I'm Phil Lipof from WCVB," he said extending his hand in greeting.

I was somewhat taken aback.

"I'm sorry my hands are all sticky..."

He smiled and said, "Oh no worries. Alain just told me your story and I am so inspired by you. I would like to share your story right before the awards ceremony if that's okay with you. As you know, I'm a reporter so I need to hear your story in your own words."

I told him about my journey with polio and post-polio and how I'd stopped running after my nephew's suicide. Alain had told him how the Boston Marathon bombings and the OneRun got me back on the roads. We picked up the story from there.

He came back and told me what he was going to share but not what was going to happen. Tom captured it all on video.

"I have a story to tell you. Mary McManus...that's Mary McManus. Raise your hand, and her husband Tom. The long and the short of it is that Mary fought polio as a child. Today she still deals with some of the effects of the disease. During the Boston Marathon bombings, she was watching. And it inspired her to get back running.

And last year Alain organized the one race..."

Alain interrupting, "The OneRun..."

"The OneRun," Phil continued. "You probably saw it on our channel and all the other channels. It was a wonderful thing. That really got Mary going and so she decided to do this race this year. And she and her husband Tom came here a week ago and did the course and decided that she was gonna do it in 47 minutes. 47 minutes.

This is the best part...Mary get up here."

I had no idea he was going to bring me up before the crowd gathered for the awards ceremony.

While Phil continued talking, Alain hugged me and presented me with a Red Sox cap with the race logo on it. He told me to put it on.

In a stage whisper he said, "Here's one for Tom."

"We sort of blocked it off but you know when you turn the corner up there, when she turned the corner she was over 46 minutes right Tom?"

"Right," Tom answered Phil.

"She had under a minute to go. Now under a minute for you to push yourself is one thing. Under a minute to go for Mary to push herself is quite another. I asked Mary when we were talking, how was that sprint? You know you're not built for that sprint anymore and Mary said to me "I was never built for that sprint." (crowd laughs with Phil, Alain and me).

"But anyway she did it and she finished in … 46 …"

"46:57" Alain finished his sentence and gave me a hug.

Alain was going by gun time, not chip time at that moment.

The crowd went wild with cheers and applause.

"It's an achievement for everyone to finish but I just wanted to point this out because this is what this race is about. This is what running is about. Mary thank you. Tom thank you."

Even though we'd talked for oh maybe 5 minutes, he got me and understood my challenges. I felt honored and celebrated but it was much bigger than only celebrating me. Today's race was about celebrating what is possible; the ability in all of us to survive and go on to thrive as we meet challenges head on. It's about having the courage to start and to start over and over again and putting it all on the line to see what we are made of.

After the race, Tom drew an ice bath for me. My adrenaline was pumping and he reminded me how important it was for me to rest and recover. I was coughing a lot from bronchospasms. Rather than interpreting the coughing as a residual from polio, I embraced it as an opportunity to clean out my lungs. I likened it to taking a car out on the highway at a fast speed to blow out the carburetor. I had a taste of metal in my mouth that can happen after an intense cardiovascular challenge. My right foot cramped and I didn't sleep well Sunday night. My legs were restless trying to recover from the race. I didn't care. I had my PR in the books. Net time was 46:53!

"I am in competition with no one. I run my own race. I have no desire to play the game of being better than anyone, in any way, shape or form. I just aim to improve, to be better than I was before. That's me and I am free." ~Unknown

After seeing the course maps for the Spectacle Island 5 Mile and 5K Race with caution zones, cross overs and elevation, and unpaved surfaces, I panicked. I emailed my favorite Race Director, Alain Ferry.

"If it were easy, everyone would be doing it right?"

He told me I'd be fine and that I would crush the course. I slept well and had a good breakfast. I'd been hydrating knowing it was going to be hot out on the course with temperatures predicted in the 80's. I was hoping for a sea breeze being out in the harbor. It was a festive atmosphere from the moment we arrived at the dock. Among the 800+ runners aboard the Provincetown II Ferry, I found my Facebook friend, Ilene Fabisch. We'd only been friends in cyberspace. She started running 2 years ago at the age of 54. She logged over 250 miles in races this year. She is a beautiful inspirational soul. She lost over 120 pounds and discovered the joy of running in her life. She was a champion and a cheerleader of my journey. We joked about how we were able to find each other without using a cell phone.

When we arrived on the Island, there were bathrooms at the Visitor Center and the lines moved quickly. We saw the 5 milers take off for their race and I could feel my pre-race anxiety begin to build.

"What if the water stops are gone? What if the volunteers are gone by the time we get there and we get lost?"

I felt the wound of lugging my leg brace and being left behind alone and hurt, fearing my little body wouldn't be able to make it home by myself.

Tom reminded me, "Mary this is an Alain Ferry race. I'm with you. You know you have nothing to worry about."

I took a few deep breaths and told myself they put 600 flags to mark the course. There's no way we could get lost on the Island.

"Just go out there and do it girl," I told myself.

Alain came riding through on his bicycle after getting the 5 milers off and told us to make way so he could get us started. The sea of runners parted as Moses once parted the Red Sea. Right before we were about to start, the front of the pack for the 5 mile race was crossing the finish line. Their speed was amazing! We broke into cheers for them.

There were no pace markers so we started in the middle of the pack. Tom asked me what my race strategy was.

"Let's go out with the pack and then see how I feel."

We started out running. I realized, given the heat of the day and the course elevation, I would fare better race walking. I was focused and running from the inside out. The volunteers cheerfully cheered us on despite the heat as they held signs with arrows. We thanked them for being out there.

The heat grew more intense. The course was hilly with elevation going up to 157' above sea level. There were very few patches of level ground. We were fortunate that for a trail race there were no major obstacles or tree roots on the course. Throughout the course I enjoyed the magnificent vista that was before us; a bird's eye view of the skyline of Boston and a view of Boston Harbor.

Alain came riding up on his bike. "Oh there you are."

He gave me a big hug and started to take a selfie with us but his walkie talkie went off.

"How are you doing?"

"I'm okay. You've done a great job organizing this race with volunteers and water stops."

"Go eat the rest of the course. I'll see you after the race. We'll take photos on the boat."

I was fueled for the rest of the race.

As we were going up the final hill, I felt dizzy and nauseous. I slowed my pace. Tom took my hand as we ascended that last steep hill. One foot in front of the other.

I looked below us and saw runners coming up the trail. We sprinted together crossing the finish line with a feeling of triumph. Before we began the race, Tom said to me that he didn't understand why I had the assumption that I was going to finish last. He was right. I finished 4/5 in my age group 60+ and 317/341 runners. There was no way I was going to PR for a 5K given the course and conditions but in essence I did PR because it was my first trail race.

John Bingham said it best, "*Our running shoes are really erasers. Every step erases some past failure. Every mile brings us closer to a clean slate. Each foot strike rubs away a word, a look, or an event which led us to believe that success was beyond our grasp.*"

I found Alain on the boat during the after party. I was soaked to the skin with sweat and an after glow that comes with conquering a challenge. He hugged me.

"I am so proud of you. I told you that you'd be able to do this race. Please remember, I will always have your back at a race."

With those words, and after conquering my first trail race, the wound that had been open for 55 years was healed. I told him how blessed I am to have him in my life and he told me he too is blessed. As we rode the ferry back to Boston, I felt accomplished, blessed and grateful to have these wonderful opportunities to feel my strength, my determination and my courage with people who support me as I find higher and higher ground in my healing journey.

Transformation at the Tufts 10K For Women   October 14, 2014

As I came down Charles Street toward the finish line, I was running on fumes. The tank was empty. I left it all out on the roads. The finisher's clock no longer mattered to me. I knew, given my splits, that I ran a fantastic race. I ran from the inside out, strong with fierce determination. Running this race was a victory lap for me after having run 5 races since June. I trained on hills, incorporated fartleks and tempo runs into my training, and did cross training with Aquatics Therapy at Spaulding Rehab. The most challenging part of training was the 5 days leading up to race day. Taper madness set in. I wanted to just get out there and run my race.

It was Tom's turn on Sunday to be in the runner spotlight as he ran the third leg of the BAA Distance Medley. I felt frustrated and sad that I couldn't be with him physically. If I would have been his support crew in person on Sunday, I wouldn't have had enough energy to run my race on Monday. The power of a spiritual presence can be far greater than being physically present with someone as I would learn on Sunday and during my race.

Tom had his eye on a PR. As I tracked him and followed the Boston Athletic Association Page on Facebook, I felt as though I were with him at the race. I could feel we had a powerful connection. I knew he was running the race for me and for us. He had a spectacular PR taking 6 minutes and 15 seconds off of his BAA Half Marathon from last year. He finished in the top ten of his age group for the Distance Medley. I was his social media maven on Sunday. Tom told me he felt my presence by his side; that he felt the magic and miracle of our marriage. He was inspired to run his best race because of how much effort and intention I dedicate to being my personal best.

Monday morning gave a whole new meaning to pre-race jitters. I felt nauseous and dizzy. It's called taper madness for a reason.

Thoughts of, "I don't have to run this race. I have nothing to prove, I can't do this," went head to head with incredible excitement and seeing myself cross that finish line with a PR.

Tom was with me, listening to my ramblings reminding me that I had trained well and this was my race to run.

"Getting to the starting line is your victory and this race is your victory lap," Tom said with encouragement and enthusiasm.

They changed the place of the start of the race and we had to line up at 11:30 seeding ourselves based on our estimated finishing times. Panic went through me.

"Mary," I heard someone yell as I came out of the porta potty.

There was Ilene!

We once again found each other without technology. We embraced and laughed about how today's weather was so much better for running than two weeks ago at Spectacle Island. We marveled at how we each had inspirational journeys, coming to the sport in our 50's. We wished each other a wonderful race. I felt how excited she was for me for this race and the goal I set for a PR.

Tom was my rock in the moments leading up to gun time. He could see my nerves kicking into high gear with this new race start.

"Let's take some photos of you to post on Facebook," he offered.

I let go of those old beliefs and instead, I let go and enjoyed posing for photos. It was time to feel my strength. I got my attitude on that I embodied while I posed for pre-race photos in the starting corral. After the race announcements and the Star Spangled Banner, the air horn went off. As I turned the corner to the start on Beacon Street I started running.

I thought, "Wait don't run until you cross the starting line," but the adrenaline had already kicked in.

"You're crushing it!" Tom said as he caught up with me right before going over the Massachusetts Avenue bridge.

I heard this voice in my head say, "Find your race pace. Find your race pace. And just stay with it."

I wasn't planning to look at the mile split times but I felt a nudge from Spirit to look at the clock.

Mile 1: 18:21. I knew that was gun time and it must have taken me at least three minutes to cross the starting line. I was on pace for a PR but there were 5.2 miles to go. Tom ran with me over the Bridge and waited on the corner for me to return cheering on other runners with his cowbell. It took 3 1/2 minutes for me to cross the starting line. I was at a sub-15 minute/mile pace for the first mile.

I walked through each water stop but never stopped. I hydrated with a few sips of each water at each stop. I had my own hydration to supplement the water stops.

Mile 2: 33:00 Another sub 15-minute mile. I continued to run from the inside out.

Whenever I felt my mind wander, I reminded myself: "Don't look ahead and don't look back. Don't worry about anyone else's race. Run your own race."

The chains are gone and possibilities abound
I'm a tree with my roots planted firmly in ground.
I'm now off the sidelines, no need to sit and whine
So much gratitude fills my heart and love and beauty shine.
After all these years I can join the loving human race
I exceed all expectations and now I set the pace.

Mile 3: 48:10 "Okay Mary, almost to the halfway mark and you're on pace."

I checked in with myself to see how I was feeling. I felt great. Alain Ferry told me that he would be cheering me on from Memorial Drive. Although I did not see him, his presence was palpable. I drew from the love and support he has given to me since I first met him at the Heartbreak Hill Half Marathon Expo. I could feel his hug at the Spectacle Island run. I remembered him willing me to a PR during the final stretch of the Bill Rodgers 5K Race to Benefit Prostate Cancer. Dr. Moskowitz and Miss Holly were with me as I began the uphill climb on Memorial Drive before the turnaround point.

Mile 4: 1:05 I couldn't calculate the split time because I couldn't do the math in my head. Instead I thought ahead to feeling the PR within my grasp with 2.2 miles to go. I wasn't going to change a thing regardless of the time. I smiled as I saw Tom in the distance as he cheered on all of the runners. He ran over the Bridge with me.

"I think a PR is in my grasp. I didn't get to see Alain but I felt his presence especially during that uphill climb after the Hyatt Regency Hotel."

I was focused not only on my PR but on the magnificent scene of the Charles River and the skyline of Boston. The cooler weather made it a perfect day to run. The Bridge was closed to traffic. The road was mine. This race was mine. The City was mine. This life is mine. Gratitude filled my heart as I experienced the gift of the present moment.

As we approached Mile 5, I told Tom the last split clock was at 1:05.

He said, "Oh my God Mary. The clock says 1:20. You just ran a 15-minute mile after being out here for 5 miles. How are you doing? Are you okay?"

We walked through the famous just after mile 5 water stop with men from the Most Informal Running Club Ever in their tuxedoes and suits. I could feel my energy begin to wane and ate the second half of my Luna Bar.

"Maybe you should take it down a notch until we get to the next corner," Tom lovingly said to me.

I slowed down long enough to chew my Luna Bar and wash it down with water and then...

Something happened inside of me. I felt this sense of strength and power surge through me. We spotted a woman struggling with her run.

I was just about to pass her but slowed down and said, "You've got this."

"I was going to drop out at mile 4 but the song, "Dream On" came on my playlist."

"I'm a survivor of paralytic polio and I'm going for a PR from my time in 2010," I told her.

"God bless you," she said.

"So if I can do this...so can you."

"You were just the inspiration I needed at this moment. Thank you. And good luck," I heard her say as I surged in front of her.

The volunteers cheered me on letting me know that the finish line was in sight. "Just turn the corner and you'll see the finish line!"

I was all alone now to finish this race. Tom had taken a shortcut to meet me at the finish.

There was no doubt in my mind that I was going to finish but there was nothing left in the tank - or so I thought.

"Maarrrry!"

Jess was about 100 feet in front of the first finisher's mat. Even though I wasn't wearing my glasses, I knew it was her. She snapped a photo of me and posted it to Facebook "Mary McManus, Bringing it home strong" with a heart emoji.

Another one of my friend's commented on the photo, "Go Mary!"

Jess Lanzoni sent me good wishes on Facebook before the Bill Rodgers 5K. We "met" in cyberspace through a mutual running friend when she was running with Back on my Feet Boston. Jess volunteers her time, treasure and talent with different running groups making a difference in people's lives through the sport of running. We became fast friends and she has been a champion of my journey. It meant the world to me to have her cheering me into the finish.

I felt a pick up in my energy even though I didn't see the photo until after I crossed the finish line.

Part of me said, "You're going to finish Mary and don't worry about the finisher's clock."

Another part of me wanted to dig deep and get that PR but my legs were lead.

At that moment I heard two screams, "L Streeet!"

I glanced over in the direction of the screams. One of the women picked up her pullover and revealed her L Street shirt pointing to it with enthusiasm. The L Street shirt I wore had a "We Run as One" and a "Boston Strong" ribbon on the back. Between Jess's loving presence and my L Street ladies, Bea and Caitlin screaming at me, I found more in the tank and sprinted to the finish. When I hit the finisher's mat the finisher's clock said 1:39:08. My last 1.2 mile split was a 15:40 pace! I knew I must have PR'ed it and thought I would have to wait to see the results. I received a text shortly after crossing the finish line:

Tufts Health Plan 10K for Women
MARY MCMANUS
Crossed the Finish at 13:37
Course time 1:35:40

Pace 15:24 minute/mile

I visualized course time at 1:35:35.

I threw my arms up in triumph, in jubilation and as a woman transformed after March 4, 2011 and all that followed in the wake of my nephew's suicide. It felt wonderful to be back in my body, to be running - to be racing again and pushing myself to the edge. I may have been alone as I ran the final stretch to the finish line but I had helpers seen and unseen to accompany me on that final leg of my running comeback.

Nine races in nine months with two PR's put a lot of stress on this body. I ignored the pain in my left knee until, after the Miss Santa Holiday 5K (another Alain Ferry race), I could no longer bear to put any weight on it. Tom and I debated about whether or not to go to the Emergency Room. We were just down the street from Mass. General Hospital where they have some of the finest orthopedist doctors on staff but we knew only residents would be available in the ER on a Sunday afternoon in December. Tom helped me hobble up the stairs to get into our home and up the stairs to our bedroom. I iced. I meditated and cried. I took a lot of Advil. I made a deal with God that I'd get an MRI and get the knee evaluated if only I could be weight bearing. I stayed upstairs and Tom attended to my every "kneed." There was an outpouring of love and support, healing energy, and prayers sent to me via Facebook.

While Tom was at work I focused all of my attention and intention on healing my knee. After the second day, I asked him to buy a cane at CVS on his way home from work. Like a dog with its tail between its legs I reluctantly made an appointment with Dr. Rosenberg. I was no longer a survivor of paralytic polio but a runner who wanted to get back to the sport that had given me so much. Unfortunately, Dr. Rosenberg still saw me as a polio survivor. He did a physical exam and suspected that I had a badly torn meniscus.

"Let's order an MRI and go from there but in the meantime absolutely no running!"

I agreed.

While waiting for the MRI results and a follow up appointment with Dr. Rosenberg, I agonized about my fate. I had forgotten, for the moment, that I had the power to heal.

"Be who you were created to be and you will set the world on fire." ~St. Catherine of Sienna

I went on line to get my MRI results before my appointment with Dr. Rosenberg in early January of 2015. The report indicated that I did indeed have a very badly torn meniscus and degenerative joint changes, bone spurs, a fatty lipoma, joint changes from multiple surgeries and fatty infiltrates into the left medial gastroc muscle as a result of denervation. That didn't sound good but I know how appearances can and are deceiving. I remembered how I dissolved a breast tumor and rewired my entire body through the power of visualization. I transcended my past. I transformed from a survivor of paralytic polio to a woman who goes the distance on the roads and in my life.

Tom came with me for me follow up appointment. I didn't betray to Dr. Rosenberg that I had already read my report. I listened as he told me the findings.

"Well we already knew you had an atrophied gastroc muscle from the polio. There's nothing you can do about that. There is not enough cartilage to repair if you have arthroscopic surgery. I can tell you in all likelihood you are going to need a total knee replacement in a few years. You know my thoughts about running. I think you know my recommendation Mary. You really shouldn't be running but if you are going to run please cap your distance. No more than a 5K. I am going to give you a prescription for physical therapy. I'd like to also highly recommend that you please come back to the Post-Polio clinic for a new evaluation. You know it's only a matter of time before things start to progress again. Don't overdo it!"

As I left the clinic with my prescription in hand, I watched myself making a follow up appointment for a re-evaluation with "the team." I wasn't sure that's what I really needed. As soon as I got home, I called Spaulding's Outpatient Clinic in Brighton. Someone from my Aquatics Therapy Class referred me to a physical therapist at that site with rave reviews. The initial evaluation with her raised a few yellow flags about her bedside manner and whether or not we were going to be a good fit.

As I was leaving the evaluation she yelled out to me, "Oh I forgot to see you squat."

I had already put on my coat and she had taken in her next patient.

"I can't squat," I told her.

"How come? Is it pain or something else?"

"I can't propriocept a squat."

"Okay," she said as her next patient stood by her side. "Go to the parallel bars and do it."

"That's as far as you can go?"

"Yes," and with that I walked to the front desk to schedule a follow up appointment.

At the second visit she donned a pair of purple sterile gloves and began massaging my knee cap and surrounding area. She used ultrasound to "loosen things up" as she explained it.

"By the way. I meant to ask you. What's up with those tremors?"

As a survivor of paralytic polio and trauma, I experience benign tremors at times. They are healing and resolving; when I'm stressed they intensify. When I challenge my body physically, they intensify. They are what they are but the physical therapist from hell challenged me about them. I quietly responded to her question while her mechanical and uncaring touch was putting me on edge. My mind raced. What was I going to do? I know I need rehab but this is certainly not the person I am going to work with. All of the other physical therapists were booked months in advance. I knew why she was available! At first I thought I should give her the benefit of the doubt. Anyone can have a bad day. I scheduled a follow up appointment but by the time I got home I emailed her and let her know we were not a good fit. I outlined my concerns. In her reply email she said that she hoped that our paths would cross again. Say what?!?

I got on my recumbent bike and worked up a good sweat. I once again asked for Divine Guidance. How was I going to rehab this left knee and get back on the roads?

I found myself staring into the deep blue eyes of 6'2" Dr. Ryan Joseph Means at my book launch party for "Journey Well." His youthful handsome face expressed his passion about chiropractic care. His dedication to the practice was palpable. We were drawn to each other from across the room of people who came out to support my latest book, "Journey Well." He gave me a pamphlet about the benefits of chiropractic care and inquired about my journey. He was enthralled with what I had overcome using the power of visualization and harnessing the power of the mind/body connection. He reached out to me two weeks after we met in February of 2015. He wanted to learn more about my journey. He did not know I was trying to recover from a serious knee injury. Dr. Ryan, as he likes to be called, didn't know that right before he reached out to me, I had two appointments with a wretched physical therapist. I never experienced a physical therapist with a total disregard for my dignity as a person. The Universe redirected me to be open to other paths for healing.

We met for coffee at the Diesel Café in Davis Square in Somerville. I interviewed him for my blog and did not know I was interviewing him to partner with me on the next leg of my healing journey.

Another earth angel was found.

"You Have a Healthy Spine"   **March 3, 2015**

Dr. Ryan Means transforms human potential into power and performance to maximize health.

"Treating you with a whole-person approach. You'll receive more than just an adjustment."

Even before stepping foot into Dr. Ryan's office, I was inspired to fuel my health and wellness journey after I "interviewed him" for my blog. The passion and the energy he exuded for chiropractic care infused yesterday's treatment. Dr. Ryan has a "green practice" where he uses a tablet for intake information and scanned the records I brought with me into my electronic record. Since it was my first treatment, Dr. Ryan began with a complete assessment including a blood pressure check, reflexes, range of motion, flexibility and palpation of my spine. We talked about my treatment goals to rehab my left knee and get me back to running. He asked about onset of symptoms, quality and duration of pain and what activities exacerbated the pain. He explained to me that there is only so much you can do with a knee joint and that it is important to address hips, feet and spine when treating a knee injury. We also addressed the importance of core strength. He had me stand and place each foot on a Theraband stability trainer. He explained how I could incorporate using them into my home rehab plan.

"I'd be happy to help you order them," he said.

We talked about my difficulty in being able to squat.

"Come over to the wall," he said.

"Most people think that a squat is down but it involves using the tilt of the hips. You'll be able to use the wall for support to get the proper mechanics and then move away from the wall when you're ready."

Dr. Ryan highlighted my strengths. He became animated as he thought out loud about what he could do to help diminish the stress on my left knee, and help me to access more energy and use of my muscles. I felt in every fiber of my being that Dr. Ryan wanted to partner with me to achieve my health and wellness best. His office was a judgment free zone. He explained everything. He educated me about the results of his assessment, recommendations for rehab both through chiropractic care and a home exercise program, and what he was going to do before he did it. I was told that I have osteoarthritis in my spine and that I was at risk for a whole host of issues as I aged.

"You have a healthy spine. The fact that we were able to hear popping sounds tells me you have good mobility and no indication of arthritis."

I was ecstatic.

I believed I have a healthy spine but after countless spinals and epidurals, and as a survivor of paralytic polio, it was wonderful to have it confirmed by a knowledgeable and compassionate physician. As he did an adjustment on my hips he made sure that it didn't cause knee pain. He reassured me that he had alternative ways to approach the adjustment if it did.

My meditation focuses on ways to unclench and to experience greater ease and grace in my movements. I imagine restoring my body to its factory settings before paralytic polio and violence. With Dr. Ryan, I experienced my body letting go. During one adjustment we heard a particularly loud pop.

"That was your rib that moved!"

I felt such relief and took a deep breath.

"The left side was more affected by polio and absorbed more of the violence than my right side. Whatever I held there was just released out into the Universe."

"Then let's leave it there!"

Dr. Ryan reminded me to drink plenty of water to flush out what was released.

After the adjustments, Dr. Ryan worked on my knee. He used this little gizmo that was painless whose "bark is louder than its bite" that reduces inflammation in the joint. He taped my knee and worked on my left foot using the Graston technique.

"Removing adhesions in the foot alleviates the torque of the leg that causes stress on the knee joint."

We agreed I would work with him in weekly sessions to get me back to the sport that was my medicine, my therapy and my joy.

Why set limits? Only take yes for an answer!　　　April 5, 2015

Last year at the L Street Pre-Marathon meeting, I was blessed to meet Dave McGillivray. I brought my copy of "The Last Pick" for him to sign.

He shared with the Club his health challenge of the past year when he was diagnosed with severe blockages in his heart.

"I got myself into this mess," were his thoughts after his cardiac catheterization, "and I'm gonna get myself out," he shared with the rapt listeners in the crowded room at the Curley Community Center in South Boston.

He explained the difference between being fit and being healthy. He went on to share with us the view of last year's events through his eyes but he didn't dwell in the darkness. He looked ahead to the weekend and Marathon Monday.

"This is our race," he told our Club.

He stood on the side after his talk. I went over to him and quietly stood next to him for a few moments until there was a lull between speakers.

"Would you be willing to sign your book?" I asked. "I ran the 2009 Boston Marathon as a mobility impaired runner."

"You did?" he said. "Good for you." He signed my book, "Set goals, not limits."

The first time I saw Dave I was at the mobility impaired start of the 2009 Boston Marathon.

"I'm going to give you the oral command to start your race. Runners take your mark, get set, go."

He put his hand down much as they do to signal the start of a lap at a car race. I was star struck to be standing next to the race director for the Boston Marathon and having him give us the start to our 2009 Boston Marathon run. It didn't matter that there was an entire race to orchestrate. He was focused and present in that moment. We were all that mattered to him. I admired his ability to put on his game face and get the job done after the events of April15th. The 2013 BAA 10K was a daunting event to put on I'm sure, yet he made sure that Boston moved forward as a running community.

We've become good friends through the years.

As Dr. Ryan taped my knee I said, "I am so happy to be working my way back to a 5K and then I'll plan to cap my distance at 5 miles since I want to run the 5 mile Ogunquit Beach Lobster Dash."

Without missing a beat, while he moved on to the Graston Technique on my feet he asked, "Why set limits?"

We are each reading "You Are The Placebo" by Dr. Joe Dispenza. He emailed me a photo of one of the pages from Dr. Joe's book while I was waiting for my copy to arrive.

"How to change the body by thought alone," was the title of the diagram. It showed the science behind how change occurs in our physiology from thought alone. I need to repeatedly remind myself about my body's tremendous capacity for healing.

"Did I tell you that on MRI it showed that the polio virus took out the medial gastroc muscle on my left calf? I'm visualizing a new one," I proudly said to Dr. Ryan.

"If I could dissolve a breast tumor, why can't I grow a new gastroc right?"

I shared the story of when, in April of 2007, I had an abnormal mammogram. Everyone told me what a wonderful oncology team was available to me at MGH Cancer Care Center. I was dealing with the diagnosis of Post-Polio Syndrome at the time and no way in hell was I going to throw breast cancer into the mix. I spent the week before I had to return for my mammogram visualizing my left breast as having only healthy tissue. I sent love and healing energy to my left breast. My mother, her mother, and my paternal aunt had breast cancer. I was NOT going to be next in line. At the repeat mammogram, they took images every which way they could and the tumor was gone.

"Why don't we tape your gastroc muscle?" Dr. Ryan suggested. "KT Tape can be used to decrease inflammation, to brace a joint and also to activate and stimulate the muscle."

I teased and said, "Mary Mary quite contrary how does your gastroc grow?"

I *am* quite contrary. I have "gone against" most of the advice I received from the medical community as a polio survivor. I was contrary to everyone in my family who were addicted to one substance or another and who subscribed to aggression against others.

As Dr. Ryan worked on my feet I said, "Wow."

"Is the pressure too much?"

"Oh no. I just went to that place within me that ran the Boston Marathon. There is nothing in the world like training for and running a marathon."

When I thought about it I felt exhilarated followed by a moment of, "I can't run another marathon." I was remembering running a marathon in my body as it was, not the body I am today, and certainly not the body that keeps changing, evolving, getting stronger and healing all that went before. I am the placebo and my body has infinite possibilities.

Dr. Ryan smiled. His blue eyes danced as he asked me to tell him more about what it was like to run Boston.

"Well then, since this makes your soul sing I'll ask you again, why set limits?"

I felt a stirring deep in my soul. The whispers of Dave's inscription in my book and Dr. Ryan asking me why set limits became a roar. Why set limits indeed? I am only going to take yes for an answer!

"After a while I looked in the mirror and realized... wow after all those hurts, scars and bruises after all of those trials I really made it through. I did it. I survived what was supposed to kill me. So I straightened my crown and walked away like a boss!" ~Unknown

"Never underestimate the power of dreams and the influence of the human spirit. We are all the same in this notion: The potential for greatness lives within each of us." ~Wilma Rudolph

I am a runner!   May 13, 2015

I am a runner. I am a runner because I say I'm a runner. I'm an endurance runner and I go the distance on the roads and in my life. When things get tough, I get tougher. I love running in perfect weather, but it's great to run when the elements are challenging because I get to show how much of a badass I really am.

I am a runner. I was told I shouldn't run; that running is bad for me. Running is my medicine and my therapy. I am a runner who feels powerful when I run. I am a runner who says what is best for my mind, body and soul. Running heals!

I am a runner transformed by each run.

I learn something new about myself in each run. I am a runner who loves a solo run, alone with my thoughts but never alone surrounded by the glory of nature. I am a runner who runs with the pack, my village, my tribe where we honor each other and practice the runner's code of no runner left behind. I am a runner who finds strength and courage on the other side of fear. I am a runner who stands at the bottom of hills feeling a flutter in my soul telling myself oh yes you can. I am a runner who stands at the top of hills with sweat pouring off of me, smiling, feeling triumphant.

I am a runner, an unlikely runner, like Wilma Rudolph who was also an unlikely runner after contracting paralytic polio.

In my mind's eye I am an Olympic Champion for running over the hurdles placed before me in the marathon of my life and never giving up no matter how tough the challenge.

I am a runner. I go the distance. I am a runner...

Loving life one mile at a time. I am a runner - Happy and free!

Armed with affirmations, Kinesio tape, meditations, faith, strength, courage and determination, writing poetry to fuel my journey and a new strength training exercise regimen, I got back on the roads. I trained for my comeback race: the 2015 Finish at the 50 on July 3. Tom was my pacer. We trained through heat, humidity, and in the evening to simulate race day conditions. He was my greatest supporter and cheerleader and helped me run my race at my pace coming back strong and steady after the knee injury that "they" said would sideline me.

The Source

Wellspring of joy flows deep within soul
rising surprisingly healing brokenness whole.
Thawing and melting magnificence made new
cleansing congestion reveals radiance True.
Miracles arise from this sacred space
fears and pain transformed by Your Loving Grace.
Running and laughing happiness free
a raucous rampage a celebration spree.
Grounded sure footed it's time fancy fine
Divine Love a waterfall cascading spine.

Fools were blind to this treasure so rare
unstoppable unceasing heart open to share.

The joy in the journey a sight to behold
the glory my triumphs I run brave and bold.
Each footstep each mile transformed and made new
a champion reborn glorious Spirit shines through.

"The secret of change is to focus all of your energy not on fighting the old, but on building the new." ~Socrates

Advice from Olympian Billy Mills   June 10, 2015

"The subconscious mind cannot tell the difference between reality and imagination ... Relive the moment the way you want it to be." ~Billy Mills Olympic Gold Medalist 10000 meter Tokyo 1964

Heading out on my training run, I wanted to break that elusive 16:00 minute/mile pace that had been with me since I returned to the roads in March. It was in my mind's eye last Saturday but it didn't happen. I'd been watching Billy Mills' YouTube video as I retrain myself as a runner. I've been keeping a healing journal writing affirmations as Billy Mills did when he had the biggest upset in Olympic history. I wanted to write in my training journal a 5K run with a sub 16:00 minute/mile pace. To be honest, I was afraid to write it down in case I missed my mark. I know you have to be willing to commit 100% to goals. I continue to clear out the messages from doctors and therapists who discouraged me from running or pushing myself. There was a part of me that didn't want to "fail" if I wrote down the goal and fell short. Although I couldn't commit to writing down the goal, I made a shift in my thoughts before I went on my run.

I reminded myself that I am a runner. I imagined Forrest Gump, Wilma Rudolph and Billy Mills. When I get out of my own way and allow the transformation to happen, I am fearless when it comes to setting and achieving goals. I thought about Dr. Joe's work in "You Are the Placebo." Instead of focusing on the how, why or what of breaking the 16:00 minute/mile pace, I focused on a PR for my race on July 3rd. I decided to set the goal and just let it happen. I reminded myself of how I felt in 2010 breaking PR after PR by setting my mind and intention squarely on the outcome.

I visualized finishing on the 50 yard line at Gillette. I ran and flowed from the inside out. I could tell when my mind strayed from working coherently with my body and I reeled it right back in. As I trained my body, I tamed my mind. I felt a side stitch and nausea, and reminded myself to run from my soul. I allowed the beautiful image of being an elegant runner within me to emerge.

I did not look at my time but had every confidence that I was running a sub 16:00 minute/mile pace. I believed it with every fiber of my being and asked the Universe to work with me to just make it happen. I have been strength training and cross training while working with my beliefs about running and setting goals. Dr. Joe writes about the importance of coherence between the mind and body. During today's run, I kept coming back to feeling everything working together. I placed all of my physical, mental and spiritual energy into the outcome I wanted for today's training run.

It happened! My fastest pace since 9/20/14 and 1 minute and 46 seconds within striking range of my 46:53 PR at the Bill Rodgers 5K in August.

46:52 is the time I want to see on the clock when we cross the finish line at the Finish at the 50 on July 3rd. I believe in setting goals not limits. I know how amazing it feels to open up this body and run as well and as fast as I possibly can. I'm back feeling strong and confident as a runner. When doubts or fears rear their head, I can outrun them. I'm retraining myself mind, body and Spirit for speed and endurance.

Success breeds success. Seeing an average pace of 15:33 with splits of 15:44, 15:14 and 15:47 (the last mile had a hill!) made me smile from ear to ear.

"The obsession with running is really an obsession with the potential for more and more life." ~George Sheehan

15 is the New 16   **June 15, 2015**

When we last left this intrepid runner, I was following the advice of Billy Mills. I finally broke that 16 minute/mile pace on my training run. Last Saturday, Tom and I set out to do our 4 miler. We knew we needed to incorporate hills and a lot of tough hills because two weeks from Friday, we will toe the starting line of the Harvard Pilgrim 5K Finish at the 50. I've got my sights set on a time of 46:52 or better. I have the course map with my time written across it on our refrigerator. I am running because in every fiber of my being I know I was born to run and born to run free. I imagine myself swift of foot like the gods Mercury and Hermes who, in addition to being swift of foot are also patrons of poets. Paralytic polio initially took me out of the athletic realm and I didn't have a chance to get back in the game because I was fighting for my survival. I am fired up, fierce with intention to allow the runner within me to fully take form.

"I saw the angel in the marble and carved until I set him free." ~Michelangelo

Why you may ask ... why is she so obsessed with running and being her personal best? What is she trying to prove?

I have nothing to prove yet I have everything to prove to myself. Tom and I talked about how we were no longer going to live in fear. It's important to be mindful and run from the inside out, but we can no longer behave as though my body is going to get injured or break down again.

Those days are over!!!

I am healing and, to quote Dr. Emile Coue, "Every day in every way I am getting better and better." Rather than tell his patients what was wrong with them, he affirmed their health and well being. He discovered they recovered from their ailments using affirmations instead of diagnoses.

I have new mantras:

Trust don't test and see if in fact that left knee has full range of motion or that the right IT band discomfort is gone. Just trust and act as if it has already manifested in reality.

Feel the joy in the challenge rather than experiencing a sense of struggle and overcoming. It's a whole new ball game now and as Dave McGillivray loves to say, "My game. My rules."

Focus on the healing not on the wound.

Feel the heal.

Focus on the wave not on the particle.

Love is stronger than fear.

I am an ambitious god.

Tom and I had an amazing run together. I ran a sub-16 minute/mile pace and my pace at the 5K mark puts me well within striking distance of my PR for race day. As I climbed into a post training run ice bath, I had a moment of pause as living in my polio/trauma/injured body briefly surfaced. How can I get in and out of the tub?

"Oh yeah," I reminded myself. "I am strong and can do squats and besides we have a railing in the tub. I am flexible and I move with ease and grace."

The ice bath felt wonderful.

After the ice bath I had an epiphany bathe every cell in my body. I am no longer victim to my body. From the time I was 5 years old I lived in fear of my body. I lived in fear of what others would do to my body but NO MORE! My mind and body work together and my mind heals my body. I love myself well and allow love to be so much stronger than fear. Two weeks from Friday I will be testing myself for the first time since last October when I PR'ed the Tufts 10K.

15 is the new 16!

You may notice my pattern of pre-race panic and the need to email the Race Director to calm my pre-race jitters.

Here is the email exchange between Dave McGillivray and myself beginning on June 29 and concluding after the race:

Mary: Hi Dave...So in setting goals not limits, Friday is my comeback race and I've been training for a PR. I'm getting butterflies and just wanted to make sure the course is well marked for those of us who run a 14-15 minute/mile pace. We went out to Gillette yesterday for final mental preparation, and have trained on Heartbreak so I am ready but just need to make sure that there will either be course monitors or signs to direct us. File this under taper madness! Thank you Dave!

Dave: There will be! I'll probably be running right behind you, too! Good luck! Dave

Mary: That's for the 5K. And I couldn't follow the course map on line. You just made my day Dave - you rock! Thank you -- it's going to be a great day and no rain :)

Dave: Oh, you are doing the 5K...I'm doing the 10K!   The 5K goes in the stadium and up and down the ramps!

Mary: I know. It was a little confusing but it will be marked or there will be course monitors right?

Dave: Very confusing on a map because most of it is in the building. It will be marked, etc. I did it last year...no problems!

Mary: THANK YOUUUU! See you Friday. Can't wait ... you are awesome you know that right?

Dave: Don't tell me, tell my wife and kids!!!

Mary: You can forward the email to them :)

Mary: As you promised it was an amazing day. Congrats on your great finish. (Dave pushed Rick Hoyt in his chair for the 10K). I manifested something far greater than a PR although I was within 27 seconds... It was a magical day. Thank you so much for allaying my fears before the race to clear the way for me to experience every moment of a very special day!

Until our paths cross again I'll be setting goals not limits - as in the Bermuda Half Marathon!

Dave: Congratulations Mary! Told you that you wouldn't get lost!!!! Ha.

My Bucket List

"You can go to heaven if you want. I'd rather stay here in Bermuda."
~Mark Twain

October 7, 2010

"When a defining moment comes along, you can do one of two things. Define the moment, or let the moment define you." ~Tin Cup (the movie)

Linda Mitchell: You are an inspiration of your defining moment Ms. Mary!

Mary McManus: Aww thank you Lady Linda -- and you were the eyewitness to it all unfolding - xoxo

Linda Mitchell: ...and you are a running inspiration...I keep wondering if I am going to make it through my first 5K, the SGK race for cure in O'ahu on the 17th and then I see all that you run and know I can!!! Someday though you and me still have some unfinished business! That run on the beach in Bermuda!!!! Or we can do the Bermuda Marathon weekend in January some year!

Mary McManus: I just got goosebumps Linda and before I even finished reading, "We have unfinished business," I knew exactly what you were gonna say -- yup -- we have to run that beach in Bermuda or better yet - when do you turn 60 girlfriend 'cuz I'm planning on doing another marathon for my 60th - you up for it? If we do run the Bermuda Marathon how oh how will I ever find a travel agent to help me make the arrangements? lol

You are gonna do great Linda in the 5K -- no worries -- you are so fit and I know you have been training and I'm so glad that you can use me for some good ol' fashioned inspiration!

Huge hug

Linda Mitchell: Wow what a GREAT idea!!! I turn 60 on August 26 2012 which I think is well before you!! Thanks for the encouragement! I have become super strong in the past year doing all sorts of training I never did! Just recently started running though but I am up for this! Let's do lunch when I get back from Hawaii and YES you let me know the date and I will find us that travel agent to help us! TEE HEE!

Mary McManus: Oh how awesome! I'll be 60 in 2013 - we are pretty close in age sweetie -- so if we did the Bermuda Marathon in January of 2013 we'd be celebrating the big 6 - 0. Whew I am so glad you can find a good travel agent - one with integrity and service and value are so hard to find these days - wink wink. I'd love to do lunch Linda -- can't wait to see photos of Hawaii. God bless you my friend. xoxoxo

Linda Mitchell was our Bermuda travel agent. After I was diagnosed with Post-Polio Syndrome, she suggested that I visualize running along a beach in Bermuda to inspire my body to heal. I didn't even know how to begin to imagine myself running along a beach so after I wrote the poem, "Running the Race," I watched "Forrest Gump."

Linda and I lost touch but I took the healing suggestions she offered me and, well, I ran with them!

Life happened and I took the Bermuda Marathon Weekend off my bucket list.

When Tom and I saw the Bermuda Marathon Weekend Booth at different race expos we briskly walked by while only taking a sideways glimpse at the inviting poster and hearing the Bermudian accents. Their booths at the Expo brought back memories of our many trips to the magical Island of Bermuda. At one Boston Marathon Expo, the representative for Race Weekend (who I now know was the Race Director) tried to stop us in our tracks. We shook our heads and hands, "No thank you."

"Have you ever been to Bermuda?" Herb Simmons asked me as I was helping him put together a photo album to write the story of the Sea and Surf Anglers Club of Boston and the Blue Waters Anglers Club of Bermuda.

Herb was the first person of color to be named Chief of Pharmacy at Boston City Hospital when, at the age of 49, he suffered a massive stroke. Initially he was totally blind and then regained some vision. He could see with his eyes but had difficulty processing what he saw as a result of the stroke. I was the Visual Impairment Services Team Coordinator charged with providing social work intervention to the visually impaired veterans at the VA. Herb made it very clear from the beginning he did not want to be a patient. He quickly transitioned from patient to invaluable volunteer. Through the Telefriend Program, Herb kept in touch with other legally blind veterans who were housebound, elderly veterans and veterans considered at risk due to their mental health diagnoses. Together we were blessed to literally save lives. I told Herb we had never been to Bermuda; we hadn't been on a vacation since the twins were born 12 years ago in 1987. He told me we must go to Bermuda for our first after twins vacation. We would take care of the airfare and our stay at the Grotto Bay, a family friendly resort, and he would make sure that his Bermudian friend and fellow angler, Lovintz Cann would be our host.

Lovintz picked us up at the airport and drove us a short distance to the Grotto Bay.

"Enjoy your evening and tomorrow morning at 10:00 am I'll be here to take you on a tour of the Island and out to lunch. Welcome to Bermuda!"

We fell in love with the Island and it did not take much arm twisting to convince us to return during a Fishing Tournament. Since fishing in International Tournaments was restricted to white men only, the Sea and Surf Anglers Club of Boston and the Blue Waters Angler Club of Bermuda started their own tournament in 1965. Their first Goodwill Tournament was celebrated by Governor Dukakis of Massachusetts and the Premier of Bermuda. The goodwill, the camaraderie and the love of fishing kept these two Clubs going for decades of tournaments filled with rituals and ceremony. The bonds of friendship were as strong as the tight lines of reeling in the big one. The day before the start of the tournament, we'd have a fish fry at the Club. We ate on the dock overlooking beautiful Hamilton Harbor.

Family and friends loved waiting on the dock for the boats to come in for the weighing of the fish at the end of each of the 3 days of the tournament. While enjoying a Ginger Beer or a Dark 'n Stormy, the excitement mounted for which team was the winner of the day and which angler brought in the biggest catch of the day. One team was crowned the champion at the end of the three day tournament. We celebrated with a buffet dinner dance and awards ceremony.

Anthony Raynor and Clarence Smith had me at hello at the Bermuda Marathon Weekend Booth at the Finish at the 50 Expo. Tom started chatting with Clarence "Stoker" Smith. I hung back but cocked an ear to the conversation. I gingerly eyed the pink Bermuda wrist bands, the bling from Bermuda Marathon Weekend races and the samples of pink sand. I glanced at Tom and felt we each had a tug at our souls. The tug got stronger with each moment we talked with Clarence and Anthony. We reminisced about when we went to Bermuda. I felt goosebumps and a warm feeling come over me, while a part of me was wondering why was I even having this conversation about running in Bermuda. Several months ago I was told to cap my distance and prepare for a total knee replacement.

"If you can get up to the Half Marathon distance, you'll be better off than running the 10K with all of its steep hills," Anthony said in his delicious Bermudian accent.

"The last time I was in Bermuda I was in a leg brace using a cane and a wheelchair."

Clarence's wife said, "Look at you now girl."

There was no stopping me now. We exchanged information. Clarence told us he'd pick us up at the airport. I chatted with Anthony about the weather in January.

"Look," he said with a deep warm laugh, "I was told you people still have piles of snow near the Seaport Hotel from this past winter. I can guarantee you this. You will have no snow in Bermuda in January."

"Twenty years from now you will be more disappointed by the things that you didn't do than by the ones you did do. So throw off the bowlines. Sail away from the safe harbor. Catch the trade winds in your sails." ~Mark Twain

It was time to sail away from safe harbor and go the distance again. This time on the magical Island of Bermuda.

"Running is about finding your inner peace and so is a life well lived. Run with your heart." ~Dean Karnazes

I'm BAAACK and It Feels So Good! July 18, 2015

Five miles in the Bank of Bermuda for the Bermuda Half Marathon that is happening in 181 days! Five miles! Team McManus mapped out a very challenging out and back course on Beacon Street with lots of hills and elevation. It was warm and very humid but nothing could dampen our spirits as we build mileage for our first 13.1 race since we ran the 2009 Boston Marathon.

There is a sense of unbridled joy and freedom setting out for a long run. Today was one of those days when I wanted to run forever. I felt amazing in my body. I thoroughly embraced and enjoyed the challenge of the hills. It's a gift to unplug and have time with Tom surrounded by green trees, feeling gentle raindrops tickle us and cool us off at times, and having time to reflect and recap the week. We visualized our upcoming race while relishing the joy of running and being in the present moment. There is nothing sweeter than the conversation you have while running with your best friend.

Cross training pays HUGE dividends especially when running on hills. I see and feel the transformation happening in my body. I experience the burn in those muscles once weakened by the polio virus. I know and trust my body has an incredible capacity to recover from a training run while continuing to heal from all that went before.

When I run and when I run long I am saying to my body, "I believe in you. We can go the distance together. Everything is healing and everything is healed. Running is my medicine that feeds mind, body and soul."

Fears melt away with the sweat. Joy and happiness bubble up from my soul. Food tastes better after a run. I feel alive, vibrant, vital and optimistic. There is a natural high that happens from the very act of running accompanied by a sense of accomplishment that I set out to do 5 miles on this course and that is exactly what I ran.

I let go of any sense of a time goal today. I know speed will come as I do speed work once a week with a 5K. I have a great training program in place. Having the goal to run Bermuda and cross that off of my bucket list infuses my training runs with determination and joy. It keeps getting better and better as I feel the heal mind, body and soul.

Five miles! I am back and it feels so good.

105

"Our running shoes have magic in them--The power to transform a bad day into a good day; frustration into speed; self doubt into confidence and chocolate cake into muscle." ~Mina Samuels

There is Magic in My Running Shoes   July 29, 2015

The alarm went off on a hot and humid Tuesday morning. Tom and I set the meditation timer for 20 minutes. I had a wonderful meditation setting my intentions for the day. I felt the love and peace in our home and reminded myself everything is rewired; everything is healed. A part of me wanted to go back to sleep for at least another hour or two but it was time to get up and greet the day. Our plank was challenging in the heat. I wanted to literally and figuratively cave but instead used my breath to power through our 2:20 plank followed by 50 crunches and 10 weighted clams. We donned our running clothes laced up the running shoes and off we went on our run.

I suggested to Tom we take a route that would give us more shade than our usual run around the Reservoir. It would give us more hills but that was the trade off for shade. Given the heat and humidity, it would have been easy to have taken an easy 3 miles and not done speed work. During my meditation I practiced my mantra: I run unencumbered. I run swift. After we ended our meditation, I told Tom I wanted to run a 14:00 minute mile.

Tom looked at me and said, "You run unencumbered. You run swift. You run a 14:00 minute mile."

The first mile had a downhill and then a fairly long uphill. We took a water break at mile 1 with a split of 15:38.

We improvised our route going into the back roads near the Brookline Country Club; a beautiful scenic shaded route with rolling hills. I pushed my pace and ran a 15:11 for the second mile. I sprinted at the end and Tom caught a glimpse on my Nike+ of a 12:14 pace.

We stopped at mile 2 for another water stop. I noticed something quite remarkable. My body used to overheat fairly quickly. I experienced searing heat behind my face through my forehead. The thermostat had been tampered with by the polio virus. Even though today was easily one of the hotter and more humid training days, instead of feeling that overheating sensation, I poured sweat. My thermostat is fixed!!! I felt strong, confident and unstoppable feeling the heal in every fiber of my being.

Our 3rd mile began with a downhill. I took advantage of feeling the ease of the downhill knowing we had a huge uphill to finish our run.

I couldn't talk while we ran; a sure sign that I was leaving nothing on the roads. I dug deep. I knew that every step I took was bringing me one step closer to resounding success in the Bermuda Half Marathon in January. We took one quick water stop before surging up the hill to our finish.

My pace - 14:18 with a negative split!

My plank was shaky. I was tired. It was hot and humid. Yet once I laced up my running shoes, I felt the magic. I felt the power and magic of my mantras. I felt the total love and intention from my partner in life and on the roads as he ran and sweated with me side by side and stride by stride. We achieved an overall pace of 15:07 today with hills, heat and humidity. I experienced profound healing through seeing in my mind's eye what I wanted to achieve.

I Ran a Quarter of a Marathon Today   August 15, 2015

There's a wonderful photo of a dog with its shadow. Its pointed ears and outline of its body looks like Batman. The caption reads, "Holy crap! I'm Batman." Perception and what we believe to be true about ourselves and our capabilities is what truly matters. I sure needed to harness superhero powers to get my run on today. It was a hot and humid 86 degrees at 8:30 in the morning.

"Why don't we plan to bring our bathing suits, park at the beach and then enjoy nature's very own ice bath in the Atlantic," I suggested to Tom.

"Sounds like a great plan," he replied.

As we turned onto East Broadway, emotions overwhelmed me as they had last week.

"Geez what is it about turning onto East Broadway that you go into a meltdown?" Tom said with love and tenderness.

Last week I had the realization that when I turn 62 in December, I will no longer be on social security disability but receive straight social security.

"It was so hard to accept being disabled, having to leave my job at the VA and all the rest of it." I sobbed and then laughed all at the same time. It was like a sun shower.

As uncontrollable tears and laughter once again bubbled up inside of me I asked, "Do you mind the fact that you could get in a 6.5 mile run in an hour but instead you have to be out so much longer when you run with me?"

"Are you serious? It's not about the time or the distance. It's about us being together."

More sobs and laughter ... "Okay I've got to pull myself together. We've got a run to do."

We started out with a nice easy pace honoring the heat and humidity. We enjoyed the water views and being out running together. I reminded myself I am free now. I am not responsible for what happened to me and I certainly did not deserve what happened to me. In the wake of those wonderful feelings, thoughts and fears bubbled to the surface. I felt my left leg tighten and swell. I flashed back to when I was injured last December; the admonitions and warnings from my former massage therapist, the physical therapists and the doctor played in my mind. I was going out on my longest run since last October's Tufts 10K.

"I AM going to run the Bermuda Half Marathon in January," I told myself.

Despite all of my mental training through meditation, I could not shake the negative self-talk. Rather than letting them be and letting them drift away, or reaching out to Tom for help, I engaged in battle. "None of you were right. I AM going the distance this time."

The next thing I knew I was flying through the air. It was as though I were moving in slow motion...

And landed on the ground ....

I instinctively knew I was fine.

Tom tried to pick me up and I said, "I'm fine. Just let me get up."

I could feel how strong I was. I was able to use my upper body strength to ease the fall. I was bleeding but it was only superficial scratches and scrapes.

Passers by were aghast. "Oh my God. Are you okay? Do we need to call 911?"

I looked pretty bad to someone who was not a runner.

"Yes I'm fine."

There were two lifeguards inside the pool at Harbor Point.

"Is that where you tripped?" and they pointed to an uneven surface on the sidewalk. "We've seen many people fall there and reported it to the manager."

They presented me with ice packs from their first aid kit.

I cleaned off using Tom's t-shirt, drank water and said "I want and need to finish this run. We've got only 1.5 miles to go!"

I felt something shift within me. I felt my guardian angel had eased my fall along with my strength. It was an absolute miracle that I did not break anything and had only a minor chip to my front tooth. I had "road rash" and scrapes but that was it! I knew the Universe was giving me a gift.

Ever since I was 5 years old, I harbored a heart trembling fear about not being able to trust in my body. One day I was a healthy 5 year old and the next minute I dropped paralyzed to the ground. Three years later I experienced horrific acts of violence against my mind and body. Those acts of violence left me using dissociation and my intellectual prowess to survive. Something jarred loose within me when I hit the pavement today. My left leg felt open and free. The very thing I feared the most happened and not only did I survive it but I went on to finish my run. I have superpowers within me. We all do. It's by totally trusting in the love of the Divine that we harness these superpowers. Even though I fell, I felt invincible. I needed to show and tell my body that we were fine after a hard hit on the pavement. I felt my strength and my resilience. I was told that I had severe osteoporosis of my hip and spine. I was warned that if I fell, I was at risk for a fracture. I took only one dose of the medication that was supposed to prevent fractures and strengthen bones. I had an adverse reaction to it. My body knew it would not serve me. Recent research has shown the drugs used to treat osteoporosis are not efficacious. I landed flat on my hip without a fracture. We completed our 6.5 miles and waded into the ocean for a cleansing ice bath. The cold salt water brought instant healing to my body. Tom and I dove in and went for a swim. We hydrated and refueled with our snacks, went in for another swim and stopped on the way home for a delicious post-run lunch at the Kukoo Cafe in Brookline Village.

I took another ice bath with Epsom salts and a hot shower. We bought band aids to protect the scrapes, and I used Vaseline to promote the healing of the scrapes on my nose and upper lip.

I used the affirmation that I use every week after our runs, "I trust in my body's capacity to recover from runs and workouts."

I experienced a deep connection to the Divine and the angels that have been there to help me create the miracle of healing in my life.

I ran 6.5 miles today! A quarter of a marathon and half the distance for the 2016 Bermuda Half Marathon. I believe with my whole Being, deep in my heart and soul that I am going the distance. It's time to take off the boxing gloves. It's time to stop shadow boxing with the demons from my past. I can settle down and settle into the person I have become...whole, healthy, transformed, and a runner girl. I claimed the superhero within me.

With today's fall I can honestly say, "Holy Crap! I'm Batman!"

13.1 Because I'm Only Half Crazy   October 3, 2015

It was windy, raw and raining sideways. 8.5 miles in the Bank of Bermuda today. Crazy right? This was the first training run that required us to don running tights and my Boston Marathon jacket, hats and gloves. It wasn't a day that invited you to be outside and run 8.5 miles on the road to the Bermuda Half Marathon but Team McManus has a training plan and we stick to it. There was a report of a possible hurricane coming up the coast and if the weather was too bad, we would have either waited until tomorrow or gone to the gym to get in our miles with an elliptical, bike and/or treadmill. While it wasn't pleasant, the weather was not going to deter us from getting in our miles.

Last year, when Tom ran the Cape Cod Half Marathon, I won a t-shirt that said "13.1 Miles. Because I'm only half crazy." I told Tom I felt a little silly wearing it because after all, I wouldn't ever be running another half marathon. Before today's epic run I had only held it up in front of me imagining what it would look like if I ever put it on. After my recovery ice bath and hot shower, I proudly put it on with a pair of sweatpants.

So this begs the question of why am I doing this? I'm 62 years old and could easily have settled for running 5 and 10k's. Why go the distance?

"Our body is capable of some impressive shit. Admire it. Challenge it."
~Anonymous

The great runner Prefontaine had this to say: *"To give anything less than your best is to sacrifice the gift."*

My gift lies not in running fast but in being able to set a goal. I do everything I can to meet that goal. I love feeling sore, tired, cold, empty, hungry, full and totally satisfied with myself after I achieve each rung on the ladder of success to my first half marathon since 2009. I marvel at how resilient my body is as I put it through the paces of training for a half marathon.

Today was a hard run with the weather conditions. I debated whether or not I wanted to get into an ice bath. I harnessed the power of my mind to get through the miles and then mustered the courage to take an ice bath despite feeling chilled after the run. I knew it was a vital part of my recovery. It was a delicious experience to submerge in an ice bath followed by a hot shower and putting on cozy clothes that claimed I am only half crazy to do this.

Every long run, every strength training session gathers and garners momentum in my healing journey. I am saying YES to my body. Yes you can do this. You are healthy, strong, vibrant and whole and my body responds with building new connections and getting stronger while healing all that went before. I am saying Yes to life. If I really stop to think about what I'm doing, it is crazy. But it's also epic, exhilarating and exciting. My journey on the road to the Bermuda Half Marathon reminds me that I am fully alive, fearless, setting goals not limits. And, after all, let's be realistic. I'm not running a full marathon, only 13.1 miles because I'm only half crazy.

"The most powerful weapon on Earth is the human soul on fire."
~Ferdinand Foch

With all that happened to me, it would seem that the fire in my belly would have been doused long ago. Yet I dug deep and kept the fires of passion for the sport of running burning again after December's knee injury. Every week Tom and I slowly build our miles. My confidence that my body could and would go the distance again grew with each passing week. Once we hit double digits I knew that with our training and the fire in my soul I was going to cross the finish line of the Bermuda Half Marathon.

Right on Hereford Left on Boylston   November 21, 2015

We'd been running around the Reservoirs near our home. I needed to get out on the open road and simulate running on a course. We chose a course more challenging than the one we will run in Bermuda with out and back rolling hills. We ran from our house to the finish line of the Boston Marathon. Today's weather was glorious with sunshine and moderate temperatures; definitely a gift for November 21st. This time last year we ran in driving snow on slushy roads as we trained to run the Boston Volvo Village 5K on Thanksgiving Day.

Running along the Boston Marathon route and once again taking that right on Hereford and left on Boylston Street reminded me of all I have accomplished on this healing odyssey. I can trust in my body's ability to go the distance. We are counting down the days to Bermuda! The race website tells me it is 54 days until Bermuda Marathon Weekend.

Don't ever let your dreams die!

"It's the possibility of having a dream come true that makes life interesting." ~Paulo Coehlo

"The miracle isn't that I finished. The miracle is that I had the courage to start." ~John "The Penguin" Bingham

December 12, 2015

It is incredibly hard for me to believe that exactly one year ago today, I couldn't finish the Miss Santa Holiday 5K because of a serious left knee injury. I waffled back and forth for two weeks about whether or not it was time for me to hang up my running shoes. I walked with a cane, went for an MRI, met with the physiatrist I had worked with at Spaulding Rehab's International Rehab Center for Polio, saw a physical therapist for two sessions and then the Universe catapulted me back onto my healing path by sending Dr. Ryan to me. We had a brief yet incredibly powerful journey together before he left to follow his bliss and go to China to practice. He reminded me about the truths I knew about the body's tremendous capacity to heal. My plan was to start training in April but I ventured out on the roads in March to begin another running comeback. While it was challenging and anxiety producing to begin again, I knew I could not and would not quit. Given the MRI results, my history of paralytic polio and childhood domestic violence that took a toll on me, the odds were seemingly stacked against me. I fired the naysayers who doubted my running comeback including the physiatrist, physical therapist, the Aquatics Therapy staff at Spaulding Rehab and a massage therapist. I surrounded myself with a village of people who believed in me.

It is unusual to have beautiful weather on December 12th in Boston. We were blessed with temperatures in the 50's, sunshine and absolutely no wind! We talked about Bermuda on our run. It was easy to be transported there given today's weather conditions. I could feel the excitement and goosebumps in anticipation of race day. We had no specific route planned. We let Spirit lead the way with pacing and the route. I felt whole and free in my body and felt that there was nothing else I'd rather do than go out on a long run.

The miracle is not that I am going to finish the Bermuda Half Marathon in just 36 days, the miracle is that I had the courage to start over again right from square one, build my base, work hard in cross training and strength training and arrive in this moment. 11.5 miles in the Bank of Bermuda - I know I am ready!

I'm So Excited: Countdown to Bermuda

One month from tomorrow we board our Delta flight to return to that magical and mystical Island to experience a runcation (a vacation that involves running) of a lifetime. The timing of Bermuda Marathon Weekend's Facebook posts was Divine. We deposited 11.5 miles in the Bank of Bermuda. While we whittled away the miles, we talked about our travel itinerary. There are only two more long runs before taper time. I have my list of what we need to remember to pack with ****PASSPORTS**** at the top of the list. Packing for a runcation is very different than packing for your average vacation. You need to make sure you have all the bases covered with running clothes for all kinds of weather and make sure you have everything necessary to ensure success on race day. I have sorted out what non-running clothes I am going to bring. I visualize myself walking down Front Street. We will return to our favorite shopping and dining spots. We arrive on Thursday. We'll head to The Rosedon Hotel, have lunch and relax by the pool. I have made our reservations for The Pickled Onion, one of our favorite places to dine overlooking beautiful Hamilton Harbor. On Friday we are going to go shopping. Weather permitting we will take our complimentary taxi ride to the beach before bib pick up.

Bermuda Marathon Weekend posted a photo of one of their beaches with this quote: *"When it's time to unwind, nothing is quite as hypnotizing as watching the ocean kiss the shore in beautiful Bermuda."*

Saturday is a rest day.

Dinner reservations have been made at the Hog Penny for Saturday night. We won't be drinking before race day but we will enjoy the ambiance and great food at the pub that inspired Cheers in Boston.

And then it will be Sunday --- Race Day- our victory lap after 9 months of intensive training. We will have breakfast at The Rosedon, lace up our running shoes, put on our bibs and head to Front Street for the start of the 2016 Bermuda Marathon and Half Marathon.

Out of all the posts that Bermuda Marathon Weekend posted on Facebook this morning, the one of a picture taken at Devil's Hole about 5 miles and change into the half marathon took my breath away. I am going to savor every moment and enjoy every mile of the 13.1 miles of the Bermuda Half Marathon. It's going to be amazing; a testament to what happens when you set your sights on a goal, combine it with intention and action every step of the way to create the outcome you desire.

One year ago at this time I was upstairs on bed rest unable to put any weight on my left leg. I was scared. I believed that my running days were over. I'd briefly forgotten all that I know and believe to be true about the body's innate capacity to heal. I almost forgot about what I set out to do after receiving the diagnosis of Post-Polio syndrome.

Sunday evening we will celebrate as I proudly wear my bling around Hamilton and we dine at La Trattoria.

My heart overflows with gratitude for this miraculous journey of transformation. We are counting down the days, adding on the miles and allowing the excitement to build.

For someone who was supposed to be in a wheelchair I run pretty fast!
December 23, 2015

As Tom and I added on our miles I would often apologize for my pace. "If you were out here running alone, you'd be done in half the time," I'd tell him. I felt especially apologetic when we'd run in inclement weather. Tom reminded me how much he loves the time we spend together on our long runs and that I inspire him with my sheer will and determination. As Tom and I prepared for our last long run on Friday, ready to run our 12.5 miles, I apologized {again} for my slow pace.

Tom said, "You know, for someone who was supposed to be in a wheelchair, you run pretty fast."

Well that certainly put things into perspective!

When I recently chatted via Skype with Clarence and expressed anxiety about being in the back of the pack, he asked me my expected finish time. I told him I was hoping for under 4 hours for the Half.

His wife jumped up and down in the background while clapping her hands (no small feat for a 70+ woman) screaming, "Praise the Lord. Praise the Lord. Bless you. I'm comin' down to Front Street to cheer you on."

Clarence said, "That's an amazing finish time! Since the course is two loops for the marathon, the volunteers will still be out there with water stops. You've got nothing to worry about."

Most of the time I remember that I am a miracle. Nine years ago I was in a leg brace, using a wheelchair at times for mobility and was told to prepare to spend the rest of my life in a wheelchair. Given the ravages that paralytic polio and trauma took on my body and what Western medicine knew about Post-Polio Syndrome, it was a reasonable prediction. Once I got still and asked for Divine guidance, different plans were revealed. Occasionally I need reminders about this miraculous journey; to let go of fear and the time on the clock and look to the heavens with a heart overflowing with gratitude.

As I post my runs on Nike+ no one has ever asked me "Well, what was your pace?"

My village cheers me on inspired by what I have overcome knowing that for someone who was supposed to be in a wheelchair, I run pretty fast.

The Universe gave me a wonderful Christmas Birthday present on 12-25-15. It was sunny and 60 degrees for our last long run on the road to Bermuda Marathon Weekend. On July 3rd, Tom and I set the goal to run the Bermuda Half Marathon. We have done the work. With one more long run, we now get ready to run our victory lap. At 62 years old I decided you're never too old to set another goal or to dream a new dream. I have made manifest what I set out to do 9 years ago: to heal my life after receiving the diagnosis of Post-Polio Syndrome.

I have finally gotten it into my mind, body and soul that it's not going to be about the time that it takes me to finish the race, it will be about crossing that finish line.

It will be a personal best because I will have achieved what I set out to do.

Bermuda Marathon Weekend: Our Arrival   Welcome Back!

We arrived at Logan Airport early and were whisked through security. When we didn't have to take off our shoes or take out the laptop or iPad and avoided the long lines at security, we asked TSA what happened. They explained to us that we were randomly selected by Delta for a TSA pre-check. The adventure began....

Traveling in winter in Boston can be dicey as we learned on our return flight but at the gate we saw that our flight was on time.

Geoffrey Smith, Boston Marathon Champion and the record holder for the Bermuda 10K arrived followed by Shawn Whalen and Mona Bisson, close friends of Geoff. Whenever runners get together it's like the instant oatmeal of friendship. Two minutes is all it takes. Just add a conversation about running.

Eight years ago when I boarded a plane for Bermuda I had priority boarding; I was wheeled onto the plane in a wheelchair.

We arrived at our seats. Tom and I were deciding whether or not I should have the window seat since I might have to get up and go the ladies room. The gentleman on the aisle said, "And I'll let you get up and go."

"Are you running?" we asked.

"No I am the race concierge," he said.

"My wife back there - she is running."

She smiled and said hello.

Before take off, I went to the ladies room. I had a moment. I cried tears of gratitude, and joy overwhelmed me. I flashbacked to my journey and all that led me to that moment in the bathroom on Delta FL 561 heading to Bermuda for Bermuda Marathon Weekend.

It was a smooth and fast flight; 1 hour and 40 minutes from take off to wheels down.

As we began our descent over Bermuda emotions once again overwhelmed me. I was struck by the beauty of the turquoise water knowing how far I had traveled since my previous descent into Bermuda.

I saw the stairs; the stairs that I could barely descend when we last visited the Island, and at the bottom of the stairs they had a wheelchair waiting for me.

I joyfully bounded down the stairs breathing in the sweet sensuous scent that is uniquely Bermuda.

I took in every detail and savored every moment of going through Customs, retrieving our bag and heading out to meet Clarence. He warmly embraced us. Geoff, Shawn and Mona stood by our side at the cab stand as we organized transportation for our newly formed entourage.

Anthony took Geoff, Shawn and Mona to the Fairmont Princess Hotel, the host hotel for Race Weekend. Clarence took a slight detour on the way to The Rosedon. He drove along the Marathon course.

"Just remember the water is always on your right. I coordinate the volunteers and we ensure everyone's safety and enjoyment on race day."

We arrived at The Rosedon and my breath caught. For a moment I was caught in my own thoughts in awe of how far I'd come since my last trip to Bermuda.

Clarence's voice shook me out of my daydream.

"You are invited to the reception for the sponsors at Bacardi Headquarters. Be my guest. The elite athletes will be there and you'll be served appetizers with an open bar."

"How should we dress?" I asked knowing that there is a dress code in Bermuda.

"Don't worry about it. As long as you're wearing clothes, you're dressed," he told us with a broad Bermudian smile.

A card from Muriel Richardson, the General Manager and award winning hotelier saying Welcome Back, a bottle of champagne with two servings of chocolate chip cookies were the first things we saw when we opened the door to our room.

After unpacking, and getting reacquainted with our home away from home, we went upstairs for tea time.

"Oh my goodness...look who's here!" Muriel Richardson announced greeting us in grand Bermudian style on The Rosedon porch.

"How are you? You look amazing. Linda Mitchell was here not too long ago. We were both wondering how you are. It's been awhile."

We got caught up on what was happening in our lives.

"I am absolutely stunned that you are here to run the Half Marathon. Just look at you...I mean the last time you were here...Well never mind all that. I will try to get out there to cheer you on to the finish," she said.

"Thank you Muriel. It is so great to be back and tea time is as wonderful as ever."

After relishing The Rosedon's traditional afternoon tea, we put our feet up on the comfortable blue lounge chairs by the pool. I listened to the Bermuda birds, looked at the hibiscus flowers surrounding the pool and the cloudless blue sky. I closed my eyes for meditation before we went off to the reception at Bacardi Headquarters.

After hearing welcoming remarks, mingling with the elite athletes, finding Geoff, Shawn and Mona and having a photo op for Bermudiana magazine, we walked down to The Pickled Onion. We arrived just in time to watch a beautiful sunset. I was sporting my Boston Marathon jacket and Altra running shoes; quite the contrast from a toe up leg brace, black tie shoes and a cane. The manager, Samantha warmly welcomed us to the Pickled Onion. After we placed our order, Samantha came over to chat with us. She was enthralled with my journey. The service and food were impeccable. Tom ordered the Bermuda Seafood Chowder. I knew it would be too spicy and too filling for me as an appetizer but I did use the warm rolls to dip and savor the chowder. I opted for a Caesar salad for an appetizer. My body felt well fed on the salmon, brown rice and string beans.

We walked hand in hand under starlit skies back to The Rosedon and fell asleep to the sound of tree frogs and a gentle tropical breeze.

When I woke up on Friday morning, I cancelled our dinner reservations at the other restaurants and made reservations at the Pickled Onion. This body needed only the salmon with a Chilean glaze, brown rice and string beans to go the distance. Fortunately, Tom was happy to go to The Pickled Onion every night.

A Bermudaful Friday: Bib Pick-Up Day

After enjoying a traditional English breakfast served on the patio outside of our room, we dressed for our shake out run. A t-shirt and capris were the order of the day. It was an emotional run realizing that I was now just two days away from fulfilling a dream I had for 3 years in my heart and soul. The last time I was in Bermuda I could barely walk down Front Street. As the waves lapped against the dock in Hamilton Harbor, a wave of gratitude and joy washed over me. We shopped for souvenirs and walked at an easy pace back to The Rosedon. We bumped into Shawn and Mona who were off to Dockyard for the afternoon. We bumped into our plane mates from Kentucky. The energy of race weekend was building. We met Chris from Germany, sisters from London, and Barbara from Minneapolis, an older runner and a physical education teacher. She incorporated her Bermuda Triangle Challenge into her phys ed curriculum.

We went for a swim. I stretched in the pool. We put our feet up and soaked in the Bermudaful sunshine. I reflected on the miracle of the moment.

After a shower and change of clothes, it was time for bib pick up at the Hamilton Princess Hotel conveniently located across the street from The Rosedon.

I tried to muster as much grace and dignity as I could on New Year's Eve 2007. Everyone was dressed to the nines wearing high heels and swanky sandals. I was wearing black tie shoes and a toe up leg brace facing an uncertain and rather grim future. It was the last time I was at the Hamilton Princess.

What a triumphant return to attend the Bermuda Marathon Weekend Expo and to pick up our bib numbers.

We had our photos taken by the official race photographer in front of a course map. Clarence introduced us to his daughter Pam, and to his grandson. Bermudians have a strong sense of kinship. It is always heart warming to experience their keen sense of family values. After we picked up our race t-shirts and bibs we sat outside in the courtyard of the Princess. Runners regaled stories of races past and hopes for what the weekend would bring. I was delighted, thrilled and over the moon excited to be among the international running community.

We had a cup of tea at The Rosedon before heading in town for our second night at the Pickled Onion.

She smiled as we climbed the stairs. "Welcome back," Samantha said. "You are now officially regulars."

I beamed.

"Samantha it says that you serve Sunday brunch. Can we please make a reservation?"

"Don't worry. I'll take care of you. It's not a problem."

Samantha hailed from Canada but called the Island her home. Hospitality came naturally to her. She was perfect in her role as manager and hostess at The Pickled Onion. While we dined, we heard the Bermuda Regiment playing as part of the pre-race festivities for the Front Street Mile. From our bird's eye view, we watched the waves of runners pouring on the speed for one mile; the first leg of the Bermuda Triangle Challenge. I felt like a horse in the gate wanting to just get out there and run. I knew I had only two more days until it would be my turn. We waded through the crowds gathered to watch the kick off race for Bermuda Marathon Weekend and walked back to The Rosedon, breathing in the warm fragrant air. I savored every step back to the Hotel that I could now take unencumbered and free. We knew it was important to get off of our feet and rest up for race day rather than stay and cheer on the runners.

On Saturday morning we woke up to pouring rain, thunder and lightning. We wondered if the 10K race would go on. We heard the stirrings of the runners in the rooms adjacent to ours. As we sat under the veranda on the porch outside of our room, runners headed to the Main House to get their transportation to the start of the race. We read the Royal Gazette, and enjoyed a leisurely breakfast watching the storm rage on. Runners returned proudly wearing their bling, soaked to the skin and laughing triumphantly at what they had just accomplished. We walked into Hamilton for lunch. When we returned, the sun came out. I felt the full effects of taper madness set in. I put on my music and put my feet up by the pool letting the calm water soothe my pre-race jitters.

Bermuda Half Marathon Race Report

We woke up at 5:45am on race day. The Rosedon Hotel, our home away from home, had a continental breakfast starting at 6:30. They usually don't serve breakfast until 7:00 but as happened throughout the weekend, everything we needed was set before us. Runners wearing bibs and members of their support crew scurried around the dining room before walking down to the starting line. This was our first international race and our first destination race yet one we imagined over and over and over again while we trained. As the sun rose over Hamilton Harbor, I felt the excitement of race day!

My stomach was doing flip flops and I was afraid I was going to get sick.

"Hey there. I was determined to find you this morning. What are the chances that we would have our bib numbers in sequence?"

I was stunned. There was our plane mate from Kentucky.

"I was on Instagram. I looked for the hashtag runbermuda. I saw the pictures you posted."

"What? I deactivated my Instagram account yesterday because I was frustrated and couldn't figure out how to use it."

"Your Instagram account is linked to Facebook so what you posted there automatically went to Instagram," Tom explained to me.

"So I saw your photos and I found out about you. I said prayers for your health last night. I wished you a wonderful run but I was determined to find you this morning."

It was a sign from God that I could relax, let go and trust my training.

The Town Crier made a proclamation for the race to begin passionately ringing his Town Crier bell. He blessed the runners and ended the blessing by saying, "God Save the Queen."

He gave us high fives as we hit the starting mat heading down Front Street to begin our 13.1 mile journey through Bermuda.

We had our race plan and went out nice and easy. We met two women at the back of the pack; a Bermudian and a New Yorker who were doing the Bermuda Triangle Challenge. We paused to take a sip of water at mile 1 staying true to our training plan. We easily tackled the first hill. I enjoyed the company of the women in the back of the pack but I needed to run my own race. Tom and I picked up the pace for our race pace and wished them well.

My pre-race jitters quickly melted away as we made our way through the magnificent Bermuda vistas. At water stops, volunteers told us to enjoy the views. The porta potties were pink and green with little white roofs. It's one big party from start to finish where Bermudians line the streets, play music and celebrate their beautiful Island. I wanted to finish with a 3:30 time, but I quickly let that go as we stopped to take photos and videos and chat with the locals. Enjoying every footstep and the beautiful views along the course quickly became my goal. Everyone cheered for us by name reading the names on our bibs. Each view seemed to be more spectacular than the one before. I had never experienced Bermuda on foot. I was always in a car, a bus or a ferry. The locals had water and orange slices at the ready to supplement the water stops. It was a glorious sunny day with shade and cooling breezes. We could not have asked for more perfect weather especially given the monsoon like conditions the day before.

"Oh my God Tom," this is just like when we trained near U. Mass. Boston last summer and we allowed our imagination to take us to Bermuda. Of course it's even more magnificent and breathtaking than we imagined."

"Can you believe we're here now?" Tom asked.

"It's really a miracle isn't it?"

When I cheered on runners at the Cape Cod Marathon at mile 10, I imagined the excitement I would feel when we hit mile 10 in Bermuda; double digits with only 3.1 miles to go.

"Whoa girl -- where you goin?"

Tom had to hold me back to leave plenty in the tank for the finish,

"Once we get to mile 11 you can open it up."

Clarence's daughter Pam greeted us out on the course. She videotaped us running just as we crested one of the hills. I didn't think it was possible that the smiles we had on our faces throughout the race could get any wider but having that moment with Pam deepened my sense of joy.

The scene unfolded just as we imagined it coming down the hill toward Front Street passing in front of The Rosedon Hotel.

I cried. I poured it on despite having just run 12 miles.

Mile 13 -- only one tenth of a mile to go.

We came running down the finisher's chute holding hands with hands held high hitting the timing mat filled with gratitude, tears and laughter.

Through every training run we imagined hearing the race announcer say, "And here they come to the finish line. Tom and Mary McManus from Boston Massachusetts. Welcome back to Bermuda!"

Instead we heard, "Here come Tom and Mary McManus of Chestnut Hill Massachusetts. Welcome to Bermuda!"

Who is going to quibble between what we imagined and what "actually happened." We imagined that glorious moment so many times at the end of our training runs, visualizing only a successful outcome on race day. We trained hard and we trained well. We were able to sail through the miles pacing ourselves, conquering the rolling hills and being mindful of the downhills. We claimed what we went to Bermuda for; to send a message of healing, hope and possibility; that the body achieves what the mind believes and of course for the beautiful bling.

I did not allow others to dictate what was possible for me. I set goals not limits. What a thrill to cross the finish line of the 2016 Bermuda Half Marathon and cross that item off of my bucket list. With a solid base of miles and training, it was time to return to Camp Hyannis to run the 10K.

"It's a sign!" a group of runners exclaimed as they walked by my table at the Hyannis Race Expo.

They picked up my medal from the Bermuda Half Marathon.

"We were just talking about how we have to run Bermuda. We are putting it on our bucket list."

The Mystic Runners from Wakefield, Massachusetts were deeply moved by my inspirational journey. In that moment of synchronicity, we became fast friends.

Paulie has been gracious and generous to offer me a table at the Expo to sell my books and inspire runners with my journey. The 2015 weekend was cancelled. It was a tough decision for any race director to make but treacherous weather conditions would have compromised the safety of the runners. I didn't give a second thought about having a table at the 2016 Expo. I was running the 10K and planned to focus my energies on the race.

A friend messaged me on Facebook. "I'm so excited you have a table at the Expo this year. I saw your name on the table. Can't wait to see you!"

I grabbed my Hyannis Half Marathon medal, my Boston Marathon finisher photo and medal, the few books I had on hand and my business cards. At the last minute, I put my Bermuda Half Marathon finisher medal in the box.

After a full day at my table at the Expo, we took time out for meditation and rest. We had an early dinner at the Roadhouse Café; the restaurant we went to for recovery after our first half marathon in 2009 and our go to place when we are in Hyannis.

The ambiance with a roaring fireplace was warm and cozy while the energy was electric. The question of the evening was, "You running tomorrow?"

What a thrill to answer that question in the affirmative.

Magic happens when I walk into the Hyannis Resort and Conference Ballroom for the pre-race pasta dinner. Even though now we pass on the pasta, the dinner is a part of the tradition of Camp Hyannis. We looked around and spotted familiar faces. We lighted upon Tony and Mary who have been faithful campers since 2009. They were seated with Bill Rodgers, Geoff Smith and Jacqueline Hansen. They invited us to join them. Mary and I exchanged a long, warm hug and we got caught up on the past two years. Tony and Mary are like brother and sister from another mother and mister. They come to Hyannis together as best friends.

The conversation quickly turned to running stories. With her quiet demeanor and dancing blue eyes, Jacqueline shared with us how she was the guide for the Olympic Trials course in LA. She knew that Shalane Flanagan and Amy Cragg were going to make the team because they asked to see the course twice. We were spellbound as she gave us the inside view of the Olympic Trials.

Bill was delighted to hear of my running comeback.

Geoffrey Smith mentioned that he was there to promote his upcoming races. Paulie invited him to stay for supper and be a guest speaker.

"I'm never one to turn down a free meal," you know.

"How are you feeling since you got back from Liverpool? You mentioned on Facebook it's taking awhile for you to be feeling at your running best again."

"I'm slowly coming round," he said in his English brogue.

He hails from Liverpool and Dublin.

Tony invited Jacqueline, Bill and Geoff to come to the podium individually to talk about about their running journeys and to speak about life as older runners. I was mesmerized as Jacqueline shared with us that she was inspired by a runner named Cheryl Rogers who ran a 2:50 marathon.

"Cheryl and I remained friends for all these years."

She went on to say, "Cheryl married a man named Flanagan. Their daughter is Shalane."

There was a collective gasp in the ballroom.

Runners were hungry for advice from these three running greats as they came together on the podium after talking about their individual journeys and passion for the sport of running.

Bill Rodgers offered, "We are all explorers. The cool thing is we are all here. Let's celebrate!"

"By the way, has anyone dropped out of Boston more than me?" he asked the runners.

Bursts of laughter filled the room.

At the table, Bill noted that a DNF (did not finish) is very smart. His message for the night was how important it is for runners to listen to their bodies.

We took our annual photo together and he whispered to me, "You run with your heart. I've always said you run with your heart."

As people asked Geoff Smith for training advice, he was quick to offer that the most important part of any program is consistency. You have to also make sure that you give your body rest days."

"Consistency is the only key to success," he declared.

He surprised everyone when he proclaimed, "The worst invention was the Garmin. Everyone is an individual and you have to figure out what is optimal for you."

He went on to say that "Running is a lifetime commitment. It's about going out and having fun. Leave the Garmin at home," Geoff emphasized.

I flashed back to Tom's advice to Amanda and Karis after their almost Hyannis Half Marathon fiasco. "Forget about the Garmin," he told them and suggested they learn to listen to their bodies, not the pace. Amanda and Karis did go on to finish the 2014 Boston Marathon.

A beautiful energy and aura surrounded Jacqueline. She was incredibly humble when she shared her impressive accomplishments both as a runner and a champion of equality in the sport of running. She fielded questions about Title IX and provided practical training advice. She shared wonderful anecdotes about her experiences as a female distance runner.

I was infused with a new perspective about running. It's a beautiful sport where each person discovers what is going to work best for them. There is no one formula that fits all and we are all explorers. This wisdom held me in very good stead on race day.

After the talk, Tom and I bought Jacqueline's book, "A Long Time Coming." I spontaneously shared my journey with her. As I handed her my blogger business card she held me in this beautiful space by her clear loving eyes.

"You know," she said thoughtfully. "There is a woman in London who is looking for women over the age of 50 who blog about their running journey. I'll be sure to give your information to her and make sure you connect when I get home to L.A."

We said good night and were the last ones to leave the ballroom.

Race day dawned with sunny skies but cold temperatures.

I asked Bill Rodgers at the starting line, "How is it with the sports of baseball or football fans can't get anywhere near the big names in the sport but here we are standing together receiving expert advice and support from the best of the best."

"That's why we are the greatest sport," Bill replied.

"Good health, peace of mind, being outdoors, camaraderie - those are all wonderful things that come to you when running. But for me, the real pull of running - the proverbial icing on the cake - has always been racing."
~Bill Rodgers

I set my alarm for 7:00 am but pre-race jitters woke me at 6:00 am. I meditated as Tom slept. I focused on creating a wonderful race day for Team McManus. Paulie called this weekend Redemption Weekend after needing to cancel the race last year. I let those words sink into my soul. I reminded myself that everything I needed would be provided for me. I told myself to trust that the course would be well marked. I dismissed an image of Tom and me being at the back of the pack with everyone taking off and leaving us alone to find our way. To ease my pre-race jitters, I had Tom drive the course late Saturday afternoon. We ended up driving only half of it because we had trouble reading the map and following the roads. Tom reassured me that he would bring the map with us. He knew where we took a wrong turn; we would take a left instead of a right and complete the entire course.

The day began in quiet. I heard footsteps in the hall and on the floor above us. It was a beautiful runners' symphony and the crescendo was building throughout the Resort and Conference Center until it was time to run. I opened up the curtains and saw clear skies, green grass and not a trace of snow. Tom and I did our plank, crunches and clams, and meditated. I channeled my nervous energy into getting everything ready for the race. I waited 5 years for today not knowing if I would ever run the Hyannis 10K again.

We went to the lobby. There was no line at the coffee shop. We ate slowly. In Bermuda I learned how vital it was for me to relax and take my time at breakfast allowing plenty of time for digestion before gun time. Friends from L Street drove down for the day. Instead of having our friends wait in the long lines to use the restrooms in the lobby, we invited them to our room. I took a moment to thank everyone gathered together, especially Tom, for all of their love and support. I got emotional as I shared how incredible I felt to be running Hyannis again surrounded by my running family.

"Two years ago at this time I was told that I would not and should not run over 5 miles and that I was looking at a total knee replacement in a couple of years. I just ran Bermuda and here I am running a 10K. I'm so grateful to you all for your unending love and support."

There were murmurings among my running family blessing me and saying how much I inspire them.

While we were hanging out just outside of the Ballroom waiting for gun time, Tom yelled out, "Hey Bermuda."

We saw one of the women we met in Bermuda. We met at the Bermuda Race Expo, after we crossed the finish line where she told us what a cute couple we are, and then again at the Bermuda Airport. We became Facebook friends. We hugged and remarked how today's weather was quite different than the weather we experienced in Bermuda just a month ago.

It was time to warm up at the start where Bill Rodgers was also warming up.

"Hey Bill. Can I get another photo with you?"

"Of course you can!"

While Tom took the picture he said with love and care, "Stay steady. It's great you're back running again."

"Well I'm going to continue to move because it's cold out here," Bill said to me. "Have a great race out there."

We started the race with our fellow L Street members at my dream pace of a 12:00 minute mile. Everyone cheered as the music blared. One face stood out in the crowd.

Jacqueline Hansen jumped up and down and screamed, "Go Mary and Tom!"

The energy of Boston Marathon Champions Bill Rodgers and Jacqueline Hansen was with me.

"Wow this feels really easy," I said to Tom as we passed the first mile marker.

He reminded me what Boston Marathon Champion Jack Fultz said. "You divide your race and the first third of the race, whatever the distance, should always feel slow and easy. If you feel as though you are going too slowly, you are running at the correct pace."

"I'm not going to look back because I am not running that way," I told Tom referring to my habit of seeing if anyone is running behind me.

Instead I looked in front of me and spotted a woman race walking. We caught up to her and started a conversation. I shared my journey with her. She shared her journey to claim her health and fitness with us. We stayed together for the next two miles or so. The course was well marked with plenty of water stops.

We were out on a beautiful stretch of the course. I could feel my pace pick up. Tom peeked at his TomTom to see our pace was 15:30. I was ecstatic and felt terrific mind, body and soul. We were following Geoff Smith's advice to run from the inside out. It was daring of me to run as my body wanted to run rather than following external dictates about our racing plan. In the distance I spotted Jacqueline Hansen jogging toward us. The expanse of ocean was to our left and this beautiful running pioneer, and Boston Marathon Champion came up on our right. She stopped to give me a hug.

She whispered in my ear," Run with all your heart."

I felt she was my fairy godmother and I was Cinderella being told, "You will go to the ball." After her hug I felt something ignite within me. My pace picked up.

A woman came up from behind us and said, "Excuse me...is this the right course for the 10K."

We told her it was and laughed. I shared with her my fear about losing our way on the course. She asked if she could run with us. She was supposed to run the half but had an injury. I had the opportunity to share my journey with her. Coincidentally she ran Bermuda several years ago. We took in the beautiful views of the course and shared our memories of running Bermuda.

Suddenly mile 5 was upon us. I had not stopped for 5 miles. I slowed down to take water and have a half of a Luna bar at mile 2 (when our bodies told us we needed to refuel) but I was running non-stop for 5 miles! I took a brief pause and hydrated ready to run strong for the final 1.2 miles. My goal was to break 1:40 for my 10K. Since my return to the roads I was running about a 16:33 pace on any distance above a 5K. When we joined the marathoners and half marathoners on the course, something broke free within me. I was running with the pack! I had a lot left in the tank and I was leaving nothing out on the roads. At this point in a race I can push hard but it's a struggle to push hard. There was nothing in the tank when I went for the PR at the 2014 Tufts 10K. It was sheer willpower to push for that PR. Today there was pure joy in my run. I was racing this race competing only against myself seeing just what this body could do.

I cried as we came toward the finish line. The sound of cowbells echoed through the air.

Paulie called out my name and said, "Just stay to the left Mary. Good job."

He was there when I finished my first half marathon in 2009. He was Race Director for my running comeback at his Charles River Run, and when I PR'ed his Jingle Bell Run in December of 2010. Today, he celebrated Team McManus with our triumphant return to the Hyannis 10K.

Tom and I held hands high as we crossed the finish line. I knew it had taken us a good 4 minutes or so to cross the starting line and the finisher's clock read 1:43. Whatever our time, the 2016 Hyannis 10K was my redemption race and one of my best times ever.

Post Race Celebration   March 2, 2016

It's been three days since I crossed the finish line of the Hyannis 10K. I'm still feeling the after glow of a magical and wonderful race weekend. Treadmill runs when the elements were too severe to get outside, cross training, garnering the running advice from running greats plus getting that out on the course hug from Jacqueline Hansen helped my pace.

After we crossed the finish line, we hydrated and enjoyed celebrating what I accomplished. For five years I sat on the sidelines as a spectator now proudly wearing the bling. Mary Kate, the woman who we helped pace at the back of the pack, came up to us after she crossed the finish line. I received a follow up thank you email from her for inspiring her. She cited how we helped her to cross the finish line in a time much better than she expected had she not met us out on the course.

I felt hungry and nauseous from pushing my pace. We entered the ballroom and my breath caught. I flashed back to 2009 after I finished my first half marathon when Frank Shorter greeted my shivering self and told me he knew I was going to finish Boston because of my grit and determination. The 99 Restaurant served post-race refreshments as they had in 2009. I once again savored their vegetable soup. Refueled and refreshed we went by the door to greet our L Street Family coming in from running the half marathon. What a thrill to be standing there having run my own race and welcome back the conquering heroes of L Street. We hugged and congratulated each other. Tom and I planned to head back to the room to shower but I was ravenous. I needed something more substantial than soup, oyster crackers, a banana and an orange. On our way to Bogey's we stopped to see our results posted on the wall.

I love walking into a restaurant after running a race wearing my bling, knowing that I am a runner and I belong among runners. The hotel was transformed from a quiet place in the early morning hours to excitement with the anticipation of gun time, and then to the joy and satisfaction of another race run. Bottles of beer, food and loud voices celebrating the day filled Bogey's. Runners proudly displayed their medals.

I received a text message from Christine, Tom's teammate on the Boston Marathon Miles for Miracles Team in 2011. The last time we saw her was when we did the OneRun in 2013. How much healing has taken place in these past 3 years. She ran the marathon relay and was waiting for her teammates to finish. We greeted each other with smiles and hugs.

"Hey where are you guys? We want to get a group photo!" read another text.

The restaurant was filled to capacity. Caitlin, the President of L Street came in to escort us to the lobby so that we did not overwhelm the restaurant with our L Street presence while taking a group photo.

It was time for hugs and goodbyes and to wrap up the post-race celebration. Goals exceeded led to more hugs and high fives.

388 18/18 M6069 1:43:31 1:39:33 16:02 Tom McManus 63 M 4405
389 15/15 F6069 1:43:31 1:39:34 16:02 Mary McManus 62 F 4404

We were last in our age groups but who cares? I was only 4 minutes over my Tufts 10K PR in 2014. I ran 6.2 miles a mere few weeks after running the Bermuda Half Marathon ...

"We had nonbelievers all along the way, and I have one thing to say to those nonbelievers: Don't ever underestimate the heart of a champion!"
~Rudy Tomjanovich

I took time off from racing to focus on cross training and recovery, and maintained a solid base in preparation for the Bermuda Half Marathon 2017. After all, I didn't want to be a one hit wonder.

Tom and I volunteered for another Dave McGillivray race, the Runners World Classic at Merrimack College in July. When they put out the call for volunteers, Tom and I said yes. We received so much more than we gave. When we arrived at the Expo, Anthony Raynor proudly stood next to his Bermuda Marathon Weekend poster with a table displaying information about Race Weekend. He told us that he decided to forego the Expo at Finish at the 50 this year and come for the Runners World Classic. I told him I would be running Bermuda again. He was delighted.

As we walked toward our volunteer station at the Celebrity Mile Tent we passed through "Charity Village." Dana Ewen Siegal was standing beneath the Voices of Hope tent. We met Dana through our dear friend Jordan Rich a few years ago watching them in a performance of "Love Letters" to benefit Mass. General Hospital Cancer Center. I met Jordan early on in my running career. To bridge the gap between my career at the VA and my new world as a poet, and author, I volunteered reading my original works of poetry and sharing my journey at Senior Citizen centers. Carol O'Shaughnessy, the Activities Director at Presentation Manor, told me I just HAD to meet her friend Jordan Rich, radio host on WBZ Talk Radio. An Activities Director by day and a Cabaret Singer by night, she had been a frequent guest on Jordan's show. After Jordan received my email and interviewed me by phone, he signed me up to be a guest. As serendipity would have it, our original interview date was postponed, and he interviewed me on his show in the midnight hour the day I ran the Corrib Pub in 2008. I was a guest on his show after we ran the Boston Marathon. I launched two of my books on his show.

The Joseph Middlemiss Big Heart Foundation's tent was striking with its big hearts with small finger painted hand prints on its logo. The Foundation was started by Kate and Scott Middlemiss whose son Joseph died at the age of 6 from cardiomyopathy. Their son Jack was also diagnosed with cardiomyopathy. To manage their grief and to channel their energies for their anxiety around Jack's fate and future, they formed the Foundation. The funds raised go to research for pediatric cardiomyopathy, to support heart warrior families at Boston Children's Hospital through social events and hospital bags for children, and to fund kindness initiatives in schools. Their son Joseph had a "big heart" and was wise beyond his years. They keep his life and legacy alive by promoting acts of kindness throughout the world.

Jeff Bauman arrived with Adrianne Haslet, and Carlos and Melida Arredondo. The media surrounded them with great anticipation and excitement. Jeff was about to participate in his first road race since 4/15/13 walking his first mile. I was blessed and honored to talk with him before he ventured out on his challenge. We had met on the first anniversary of 4/15 at his book signing for "Stronger" at Fenway Park where I shared my journey with him. He was moved to tears while looking at me in disbelief to hear what is possible after trauma. When I told him I was still running strong and had run the Bermuda Half Marathon in January, he beamed.

"You know I'm really nervous about doing the Celebrity Mile," he shared with me.

"With all the love and support surrounding you Jeff, you are going do great but I totally understand your jitters."

David Brown, former meteorologist for Channel 5 in Boston and now Chief Development Officer for Mass. Association for the Blind (an agency I frequently used for my veterans) was part of the Celebrity Mile along with friends Amby Burfoot, Steve Cooper, Becca Pizzi and John Young who have been inspired by my running adventures. We greeted the celebrities, handed them their swag bags with t-shirts and bibs and snapped a few selfies. Boston Police Commissioner Bill Evans was incredibly generous with his time. He repeatedly thanked the volunteers while we thanked him for all he has done to keep our City safe. I was honored and humbled to meet Martin Richard's father, Bill who also thanked us for all we did. He beamed with pride to have a solid representation of Team MR8 at the event. He established the Foundation to honor his son's legacy of kindness and peace, and to encourage health and fitness among our youth at the event. I got goosebumps when I saw them gathered before the Celebrity Mile. Bill received several minutes of applause during the introductions.

We sent the celebrities off in grand style. After we saw the celebrities run the first loop, we headed toward the finish line. The crowd went wild as Jeff, Carlos and Melida came toward the finish line.

Dave had us clear a path saying, "He has one more lap to go," and Jeff echoed while intently focusing on his steps, "I have one more lap to go."

Dave encouraged the celebrities and volunteers to walk the 2nd lap with Jeff. Talk about magic!

Three years ago Carlos pushed Jeff in a wheelchair and saved his life. Today Jeff pushed Carlos, who was recovering from foot surgery in a wheelchair across the finish line.

As Dave said in an interview after the event, "It could not have been scripted better."

The whole day could not have been scripted better as we walked as a Boston Strong community celebrating healing, resilience, strength; as a community that pays it forward through running and weaves a tapestry of love that only gets stronger with greater resolve in the face of an act of terrorism. As the brilliant July sun shined upon us, we as a community brightly shined our light.

In August, Team McManus increased miles with our eyes on the prize: the Bermuda Half Marathon 2017. Mother Nature was not as kind to us as she had been during our 2015 training season. The weather conditions helped me to mentally prepare for what was to come on race day.

As the miles increased, so did my anxiety. Even though Anthony reassured me that I need not be concerned about the new four hour time limit for the Half Marathon, whenever I thought about that statement from the website, I felt that old clutch of anxiety. The wound of being left behind lugging my leg brace reopened.

We pondered and pondered and pondered some more ...
we pondered and pondered til our puzzler was sore.
The forecast for rain and 12 miles we must run
it's Christmas Eve will Team McManus get it done?
With water and fueling a trash bag or two,
Team McManus decided there was only one thing to do.
A little rain won't hurt us we're hearty what's more....
after today's run there's Christmas and taper time in store.
With Altras and Brooks we're layered answering the call
Now dash away dash away dash away all!

Twenty days until Bermuda Marathon Weekend 2017.

One more long run to go.

The weather forecast was for sunshine today. It was tempting to wait to get in our last long run but we would have missed out on a magical Christmas Eve run had we waited for the sun to shine. It was only drizzling when we started out on our last 12 mile run. We put on trash bags because the forecast was for steady rain throughout the day. We had a game plan. We'd have our water and refueling in the car. There was a Starbucks nearby for pit stops to warm up and take a break from the rain if needed. We'd park and then run 8 times around the Reservoir.

During our first loop we bumped into several friends who were also out on a training run. One of them was training for her first marathon in May. I gave her a pep talk. I said that it's "all up here" referring to the power of the mind. The puddles and mud became quite formidable by mile 4.

"Hey how about after our next loop we run down Beacon Street. The buildings will provide some protection."

"Sounds like a plan," Tom answered.

And then I got an idea - an awful idea - a wonderful awful idea to quote "How the Grinch Stole Christmas." Why not stop into Marathon Sports Brookline to purchase dry socks and gloves and make a pit stop?!

We were warmly welcomed by Will, one of our running and Marathon Sports family friends and the store manager Katie. Will attended to us as one attends to ultra runners at an aid station. He anticipated our every need and selected the merchandise we needed off the rack.

"What socks are you wearing Mary? Oh those are Balega Enduro. Do you care what color? What size are you? We don't have waterproof gloves but these will keep you warm. We still need gloves for Tom. Tom what socks are you wearing? Are those compression socks too tight ... we can get a different size."

They let us leave our wet gloves and socks in a Marathon Sports bag to pick up on our way back. They gave us high fives and told us "You got this!"

A few blocks later, we bumped into our dear friend, Paula who works at Party Favors on Beacon Street. Her husband is an Emergency Responder who ran the right way and attended to those affected by the bombings on that fateful Marathon Monday. We met on One Boston Day on 4/13/15. It was a day to celebrate resilience and to declare that 4/15 would become a day of service for the City of Boston. We chatted as we made our way down Beacon Street. We left her as she went to buy a last minute gift before heading back to work. Tom told her he would see her later in the day to pick up my cake. As we wished each other Merry Christmas and Happy Birthdays (hers was a few days ago and her son's is Christmas Day) we hugged tightly.

"Please send our love and gratitude to Walter," I said as we parted ways.

Tom and I made our way down Beacon Street pausing a couple of times to take shelter on the porches of apartment buildings. We laughed so hard as we imagined ourselves getting arrested for loitering. As soon as our mileage hit 8 miles we turned around. We were warmly welcomed back to Marathon Sports as we refueled, hydrated, and made a pit stop. It's amazing how much you have to pee when you run in the cold wet weather especially when you're laughing so hard at what you are doing to get in a training run. Katie put the Marathon Sports bag into Tom's running backpack. More high fives and cheers as they sent us on our way. We expressed our deepest gratitude for all the care and support they gave us.

We made our next mile pit stop at Starbucks in Cleveland Circle. I was ready to bail as we hit 10 miles but instead decided to heed the advice I gave to our friend about "it all being up here." We were soaking wet. Our shoes squeaked. Yet I knew I could not quit before 12 miles. I knew I needed to mentally prepare for Bermuda in case the going got tough at any point in the race. I had never put my body through the rigors of training for 2 consecutive half marathons. In the back of my mind I thought about my friends sharing in our training journey on Facebook. They would have completely understood if I would have quit at 10 miles. Something deep within me urged me on to finish the 12 miles.

"It's a great day for a run...in the rain...while everyone waits for sunshine, you have the roads all to yourselves," he said to us as we attempted to warm up inside Starbucks.

I noticed his dog tags. "Are you a veteran?"

"No I'm active duty."

"Army?"

"No Marines."

"Semper Fi." "I worked at the VA as a social worker for almost 20 years."

"My dad worked at the VA as a psychologist."

"Oh? What was his name?"

"Last name? - Eisenberg."

"Oh my God," I said. "Mark Eisenberg? I worked with him at the Causeway Street Clinic."

"Well that's what the holidays are all about," John said to us. "Making new friends, connecting with old friends and bringing warmth to everyone you meet."

And with that we went on to finish our run. The rain slowed. The day got brighter. By the end of our 12 miles, the sun poked through the clouds!

Let taper madness begin as we countdown to Bermuda Marathon Weekend. I celebrate the gift and miracle of my life on my 63rd birthday, having 12 magical Christmas Eve miles in the books.

"The celebration of success overshadows the challenges that were encountered along the way." ~Jeffrey Benjamin

Bermuda Marathon Weekend 2017

Tom decided to take on the 2017 Bermuda Triangle Half Challenge. I spectated the Front Street Mile and cheered him on to a stunning finish at a 7:59 pace Friday evening. On Saturday I stayed at The Rosedon Hotel eagerly waiting his return from the Bermuda 10K. I waited on the bench where I once sat in a leg brace facing a grim and uncertain future. While I wore a party hat ushering in that New Year I felt anything but festive and hopeful. I reflected on the miracle of my journey. While I ushered in a new era in my life, it was the end of an era at The Rosedon Hotel.

Tom returned proudly wearing his bling from the second leg in his Bermuda Triangle Challenge.

"How was it?" I asked.

"Just as hilly as advertised but I had a great time. I helped Shawn make it to the finish. He was hurting but you know how much he fights the pain."

The Friday after Race Weekend, Shawn was scheduled for a 3 D total knee replacement. He went out in style and planned to return to the sport he loved since high school after he recovered from the surgery.

The Rosedon was under new management getting ready to close for a few months for renovations. There was a retirement party for our dear friend Muriel, and staff we had known through the years. Muriel invited us to join the luncheon. We reminisced about our many trips to The Rosedon. Muriel fondly remembered when the Sea and Surf Anglers Club took over The Rosedon. Beau, one of the iconic figures of The Rosedon prepared a fish fry with their catches from the tournament. The entourage of the fishing club members along with friends and family, sat around the pool until long after sunset imbibing on Dark 'n Stormy's. They would get up at sunrise yelling to one another across the garden. She shared in our sadness for the loss of many Bermudian and Bostonian anglers including my beloved friend Herb Simmons.

Music, great food, gift bags for outgoing staff, balloons and tissues filled the porch of our beloved Bermudian hotel.

I couldn't linger in my feelings for what was happening at The Rosedon. I was grateful we had the opportunity to say farewell to Muriel and staff we had known for many years. I had a Half Marathon to run on Sunday.

I used to lament the fact that I couldn't keep pace with the pack and had to carefully choose what races I participate in. During my meditation by the pool, I had the epiphany that I was not trailing behind anyone. I am a trailblazer with courage to defy what the medical establishment told me about Post-Polio Syndrome. "If you use it you will lose it!"

That epiphany receded into the background after the gun went off for the 2017 Bermuda Half Marathon.

"When your legs can't run anymore - run with your heart." ~Anonymous

"And let us run with endurance, the race that is set before us." ~Hebrews 12:1

I posted a picture on Facebook that I was rereading Jacqueline Hansen's book, "A Long Time Coming," to inspire me for race day.

"A perfect way to manage taper time. I'm reading about inspirational pioneers in women's running. Poignant since Joan Benoit Samuelson is running this weekend. It's my second reading and must say it's even more enjoyable the second time around!"

Jacqueline, who was gracious to write the Foreword to "Going the Distance: The Power of Endurance," posted:

"Thank you Mary! I loved that Joanie wrote my foreword, and now I have written yours. Have a good race, stay the course and, as always, run with heart. Love, JQ"

I replied, "Will do."

Little did I know how much I would have to run with all my heart to get to the finish line.

It was a gorgeous morning in Bermuda. We were once again treated to the beautiful sunrise over Hamilton Harbor. I experienced the thrill of supporting Tom in his Bermuda Triangle Half Challenge races and now, Team McManus was ready to take on my second Bermuda Half Marathon. I was stronger and trained harder than I had a year ago. I remembered to be mindful as I ate my breakfast. We had our breakfast earlier than last year to give me time to digest it before the start. We left for the start later than we had last year. Unlike last year, I felt pure joy before gun time.

We met Thomas Glave in 2016. He decided to take on the Bermuda Triangle Half Challenge this year after running the Half last year. His eyes filled with tears as he told me how much I inspire him.

"If I hit a rough patch during the race, I am going to use the mantra, "Remember Mary Remember Mary and all she's been through."

"Hi Mary. It's Glenda from last year. You were kind to send me the photos from the start last year. I looked you up and was so inspired by you that I'm taking on the Half Challenge this year," she said as she proudly showed me her bib.

After the Proclamation from the Town Crier, we crossed the timing mat for our second consecutive Bermuda Half Marathon. Thomas asked if he could join us for the first few miles to warm up.

"Hey Mare, I think we're going too fast," Tom said with concern.

"No I feel great," I told him. "I don't feel like I'm pushing my pace at all."

"Yeah but we're doing a 16 minute mile and change."

I ignored his warning.

In the back of my mind I was going to run a sub 4 hour half marathon.

We paused at mile 1 to take a sip of water and then took the first hill. We chatted and sailed through the first 6 miles taking in the uniquely Bermudian landscapes and, after mile 5, the magnificent seascape. The conversation and the run were delightful except when cars whizzed by us. I had no pain anywhere in my body. The water stops were fewer and farther between than last year. We made sure to stop at the water stops but unlike last year, I did not stop to chat with the locals. I could feel that internal pressure of the clock ticking and I wanted to break 4 hours.

"Hi Mary. I told you I'd be here," said a Bermudian woman who I met while cheering on Tom at the Front Street Mile.

She used to run despite having a foot that turned inward but she sustained an injury and was now unable to run. We had a lovely chat at the Front Street Mile. Strangers quickly become friends in Bermuda. She embraced me knowing my story and told me to take plenty of water and have an orange slice.

"Hello Mary's husband," she said to Tom.

At mile 6 Thomas peeled away from us and went on to run his own race. Because we were chatting with Thomas, I was not paying close attention to my hydration and fueling plan especially as the day warmed up. We remembered spectators who lined the route last year and they remembered us. The reggae music accompanied the magnificent views of the Island. It was a dance party. I anticipated a smooth and easy run but as any endurance runner can tell you, things can often go south when you least expect them to. I trained well on hills and asphalt this year. I incorporated more cardio into my training using the Arc Trainer and Bike. I increased the intensity of my strength training workouts on land and in the pool. Unlike last year, and my hunch is because the America's Cup was coming to Bermuda in June, there was a lot of traffic on the roads. We had to hug the left side of the road where the road had uneven pavement. I felt my gait was off kilter. We resumed our hydration and fueling plan. Fortunately, in addition to the two water bottles in our fuel belt, we had brought a bottle of Fuji water from The Rosedon. Tom and I shrugged off the fact that there seemed to be more traffic this year although it was beginning to take its toll on me. We reminded each other to focus on enjoying the race.

Enjoyment of the race shifted to surviving the race as the miles wore on.

"Are you favoring your left side?" Tom asked me with a worried tone when we got to mile 9.

"It's from the road angle," I said. "I'm doing fine. I'm not in any pain."

The right side of my back went into spasm with the long hill between mile 9 and 10 combined with the the heat from the sun. I massaged the spasm. I told myself, "I am confident and comfortable in my body."

I embraced what was happening to my body. By mile 10, I felt a release and said a prayer of gratitude that the tightness was gone.

Between miles 10 and 11, I could feel the toll that the fast start, the heat, the hills and having to negotiate traffic was taking on my body. I harnessed the power of my mind to think, in the words of Dr. Joe Dispenza, greater than my circumstances. I observed my body rather than embody the spasms which could certainly have sent off a wave of panic within me.

We stopped and stretched and made sure we had plenty of hydration. While I would experience moments of relief, they were short lived and far between. I harnessed the power of the mantra that I have used before in my runs if a part of my body was experiencing pain or swelling. "I created this so I can uncreate it."

Shortly after mile 11, I had a mystical encounter with one of the volunteers.

He got right in my face and said in his rich Bermudian accent, "The race is not for those who are swift. The race is for those who can endure. You're the winner. You can do this. Now go finish."

He released the two hands he had placed on the side of my arms. His preaching infused me with strength and positive energy. I reassured him that I was going to finish the race set before me.

Last year there was no marker for mile 12. It didn't matter because I was sailing through the final miles of the race. We knew we were coming close to the finish. This year I was so relieved to see the sandwich board in pink and blue colors that told me I made it to Mile 12. With only 1.1 miles to go I knew I was not going to quit. The question was how was I going to finish? I had to accept the fact that I was listing to my left side. My left arm was in spasm. I lost muscle control over my upper body. We stopped and stretched every which way I could think of to get relief and hydrate.

"Are you okay? Do you need water?" a beautiful runner said with a delightful British accent.

"No we have enough water...I'm stretching trying to work out cramps. Thank you."

As we turned the corner I welcomed the downhill heading into Front Street. One foot in front of the other was all I could think about. At the wall in front of The Rosedon, a spot where I felt incredible triumph in 2016, I was losing control over my entire body. Tom supported me as my body melted down toward the ground. I dumped water on my head, took a big gulp of water and pulled myself together. I had to block out the trigger that was happening inside of me from the day I collapsed in gym class after contracting paralytic polio.

Tom had the brilliant idea of having me put one arm around his shoulder while he braced my hip. As we moved slowly toward the finish line, the angel from mile 12 appeared.

"Come on. Put your arm around me. I'm going to help you."

She could tell I was stunned. "They did it for me when I cramped up in Chicago and Philadelphia actually. It's okay. This is what we do for each other."

With Tom and the earth angel from mile 12 flanking me on either side, I powered up Bermudiana Road and then down the final hill toward the finish line.

I kept saying thank you amidst the conversation we shared to keep me distracted from what was happening in my body. I cried and shared my story. She reassured me that I would finish this race. She acknowledged my strength and my courage. She told us a bit about herself and her running comeback after a slipped disc. Tom and our earth angel kept me focused on my single minded goal: to cross that finish line.

"I'm going to step aside right before the finisher's chute so I'm not in your finish photo," this angel said to me.

I was never so happy to see a finish line in my life! As we planned and visualized so many times, Tom and I had hands held high (even though I was leaning to my left) with huge smiles on our faces. We celebrated that I ran my second consecutive Bermuda Half Marathon. It wasn't pretty but I got it done.

As soon as we crossed the finish line, I was greeted by medical tent volunteers. "Come in here and let us check you out," they said.

Tom insisted.

"Wait," I said with outstretched arms for emphasis before I'd take another step forward into the medical tent.

"Where are our medals?"

"I'll go see about them," Tom said. "Sit down and let them check you out."

While the medical tent staff checked my blood pressure, blood sugar and oxygen levels, Tom came back to tell me they ran out of medals. My first thought from days gone by was I was too slow and missed out. We found out that a shipment of medals had disappeared and never arrived in Bermuda. I suggested they must have gotten lost in the Bermuda Triangle.

"Here drink this," one of the medical tent personnel said to me handing me a bottle of Gatorade.

I took a few sips and then asked for water. As I started to guzzle the water she pulled the bottle away from me.

"You need to take small sips. I don't need you throwing up in my medical tent."

"Could I please have some ice for my knees?"

"No. Here wrap this foil around you. We don't want you getting hypothermia."

"But I'm from Boston. I'm actually quite hot."

"This is the protocol we follow here. Now take some deep breaths and relax."

I allowed myself to be ministered to by the EMT's and smiled to myself. "There's a first time for everything," I thought. "This is the first time I've ever ended up in a medical tent and was almost a DNF."

Tom forgot his wallet to pay for brunch at the hotel so while I was being attended to, he ran back to The Rosedon to get it. As soon as I sat down on the cot, I felt everything release. I was amazed at how I was unafraid about what happened during the race, and had total confidence in my body's ability to make a rapid and complete recovery. Vital signs were fine including blood sugar. One of the medical personnel told me I fueled and hydrated well based on my rapid recovery. While sitting on the cot, I willed myself to recover quickly not wanting to end up in a hospital in Bermuda.

My angel, whose name is Jamie-Lee Wright, came back to check in with me after I left the medical tent. She had a stellar running comeback at the Triangle Half Challenge after 6 months of not running. She trained for only 6 weeks prior to race weekend. After she PR'ed her half she went back to her house which is along the race course to cheer on a friend running the full marathon. He was struggling and she ran him to the finish. After she helped him to cross the finish line she came to find us to help me finish.

"It's really no big deal," she said. "I saw how much you were struggling and I wanted to see if there was anything I could do to help."

It was time to celebrate and get our party on after crossing the finish line and triumphantly emerging from the medical tent.

We ate brunch at the Pickled Onion where Jamie-Lee and the Bermudian running group, The Weekenders were also celebrating their races. Although Samantha wasn't in Bermuda for race weekend to prepare two bags of ice for me after the race, the manager had instructions from her to bring me two bags of ice while we enjoyed our brunch.

I hobbled up the stairs after having our picture taken with the Town Crier. On the Bermuda Marathon Weekend website, there are photos of runners having their picture taken with the Town Crier proudly displaying their medals. I had that moment seared in my imagination and knew I wanted to create that moment after we crossed the finish line of the 2016 Bermuda Half Marathon. Samantha was at the top of the stairs to greet us and led us to a table overlooking the finish line where we cheered on the Marathon finishers. After we ordered avocado egg rolls and sparkling water for me, and an omelette and coffee for Tom, Samantha brought over two bags of ice lovingly prepared with linen tourniquets to hold the ice. I cried when she presented them to me.

"Congratulations on an incredible journey," she said as she bent over to give me a hug and take a closer look at my medal.

After our 2017 celebratory brunch, we took a very leisurely walk back to The Rosedon. After a nap, we showered and took a cab to the Fairmont Southampton Princess Hotel for the race after party. As we mingled with running greats Geoff Smith, Bart Yasso and Joan Benoit Samuelson, we greeted running friends from the States and Bermuda. We danced, dined on delicious food and shared race stories past and present. Although I had no bling to show for my efforts, I felt jubilant and radiant. The music was provided by the Town Crier and his band. He smiled broadly when he saw us take the dance floor.

We had one more full day in Bermuda before returning to Boston. To celebrate my 10 years of healing, we booked an extra day in Bermuda this year. Little did I know how much we were going to need the extra day to recover from what turned out to be a grueling, yet magical and mystical race day for me.

Prior to race day, we stuck with our fueling plan for breakfasts of oatmeal, banana, orange juice and toast. We brought in our oatmeal and shopped at Miles Market to get bananas. After our triumphant race, we ordered the full English breakfast delivered to the porch of our room. We feasted on bagels and lox with capers, an omelette with breakfast fruit, and The Royal Gazette with a recap of the weekend's race festivities. After a rain shower, the sun came out. We took advantage of The Rosedon Hotel's complimentary cab to Elbow Beach on the South Shore.

As the woman handed us our complimentary beach towels, she said, "Welcome to Paradise."

I bathed in the warm turquoise waters and allowed the powerful surf to help me recover from my race. We took a recovery walk on the pink sand. We sat with our feet up on lounge chairs covered with luxurious towels reading for a few hours. There was a brief shower but as they say in Bermuda, "Not a problem." We put up our beach umbrella until the sun came out again. At 1:00 pm our courtesy ride took us back to The Rosedon. We went for a recovery swim in the hotel pool, showered, and had our last tea time on the porch with friends we made during our stay. We shared stories about our weekend races, races of days gone by and "what's next" on our racing calendar. Tom and I took a leisurely walk into Hamilton to shop for gifts for our dear friends who were house and cat sitting for us.

"Can we walk over the route for the finish of the Half Marathon?" I asked Tom.

His initial response was a curt no. He was worried about my recovery and going up yet another hill. He quickly recanted and said, "Of course."

He instinctively knew I needed a "do over" from the end of Sunday's race. It felt so good to be walking under my own steam noticing how quickly my body recovered from the rigors of race day. It was a true testament to how far I've come in these past 10 years since first receiving the diagnosis of Post-Polio Syndrome with warnings that I would be experiencing a progressive neuromuscular disease. It's a testament to my training hard and to reclaiming my life from the effects of paralytic polio and trauma through the power of visualization, intention and effective action.

Many people asked me why I don't just take a regular vacation now that I feel well enough to travel, eating the full English breakfast every day, going to the beach and lounging by the pool. The people who ask me that question are not runners. There's something incredibly wonderful about training for 6 months, exercising discipline, honing mind, body and Spirit to take on 13.1 miles and then reaping the rewards from that hard work. The joys of savoring great food, enjoying the sunset with our view from the Pickled Onion patio and a glass of wine after lounging on the beach and by the pool are so much sweeter after crossing the finish line. I can't imagine life any other way.

From "Easy Out Alper"....

On one of our long runs, early on in my adventures as a runner girl, I had an image of my polio self and who I am today side by side in a bubble. As I ran, the bubble got longer and longer until the bubble finally burst. I was free. I felt God's presence as a long forgotten childhood memory surfaced. I vividly remembered one day in gym class. We were playing kickball and the entire outfield moved in as they always did when I was up at the plate. The pitcher rolled the ball. Wham! I connected with the ball. I had a moment of shock and then limped around the bases as fast as I possibly could. I ended up scoring a home run because there was no one in the outfield to play the ball and get me out.

In that moment, I learned how anything was possible.

Despite that home run, I continued to carry the nickname of "Easy Out Alper" and was always the last person picked for a team in gym class.

I could have looked upon my 2017 Bermuda Half Marathon race experience as something that could happen to any runner. I hit the wall, cramped up and my body just shut down. However, those moments from mile 12 to the finish line became a profound mystical experience for me. The fear that I could collapse and have no control over my body happened. Instead of allowing fear and panic to crush me, I dug deep and moved beyond the fear from my past. I harnessed the power of myself as a 63 year old woman and put into practice the wisdom I garnered during my healing journey. The deep wounds of having been bullied, teased and left behind while I was left lugging my ankle to hip metal leg brace were Divinely transformed as Jamie-Lee came to find me. Her support, reassurance and care for me as one cares for one's dearest loved one transformed those memories and healed the wounds from the past. It was the runner's code in action. I went from being "Easy Out Alper" to a woman celebrated and honored for being a source of inspiration. Jamie-Lee shared my story with The Weekenders gathered post-race at The Pickled Onion. Our story is now part of Bermuda Marathon Weekend history. There was no bling to wear at the airport but I carried a treasure deep inside of me. A wound was healed and new friendships forged that will last a lifetime. I pushed myself and tried to outrun my past by setting a time goal for myself rather than embrace the miracle and wonder of the gift of healing in my life.

I planned to run the Hyannis 10K again in 2017 but I knew I needed time to recover from Bermuda. Paulie gave me a table at the Expo. I gave Frank Shorter and Bill Rodgers a copy of my book, "Going the Distance: The

Power of Endurance." They were inspired and moved to know how much they inspired me on the roads and in my life. Tom ran the Hyannis Half Marathon and PR'ed it. We enjoyed a perfect Camp Hyannis Weekend. My table was the hub of activity and a magnet for my friends to come visit with me sharing in my triumphant Bermuda Half Marathon run.

As we drove across the Sagamore Bridge returning home after back to back running vacations, I reflected on all that I had accomplished in my healing and running journey.

My heart swelled with gratitude. Tom and I talked about my next goals in life and on the roads. We reflected on the changes at The Rosedon, shared our disappointment in the lack of road closures and respect for the runners during the Half Marathon and a shift in the vibe of the Island with the impending arrival of the America's Cup Challenge. We toyed with changing our running vacation destination to Key West for January 2018 or to look for other Half Marathon destinations for the Fall of 2018. My personal goals were to continue blogging, inspiring people with my message of healing, hope and possibility on social media and to find opportunities for public speaking.

From February to April, I settled into a training routine of swimming, cardio, strength training and feeling good running at shorter distances. We signed up for a Paulie race during Memorial Day Weekend; an all pace race in Hyannis. Our friends were gearing up for another training cycle for the Boston Marathon. Our Saturday runs dovetailed with those running on the Boston Marathon course.

April 8, 2017

Tom and I returned to Heartbreak Hill to get in a 5 mile run. The energy and excitement leading up to the Boston Marathon weekend was electric. Runners were getting in their last shake out run. The stored energy for taper madness was palpable.

One runner said, "Thank you for the smile."

Everyone was asking each other, "You running?" We did not even need to finish our sentences with "Boston this year."

Tom and I reminisced about our training runs on Heartbreak Hill and the magic of April 20, 2009. The moment when Domenick told me to go get my medal is forever imprinted on my heart and soul. We fondly recalled when Janine waited for us at the top of Heartbreak Hill to run with us to the finish line. When we spotted her in the distance, she shifted from side to side bracing against a stiff headwind trying to keep warm. She wrapped her cold hands around her pulled down long sleeve white t-shirt that she wore underneath the blue Spaulding Rehab "Street Team" shirt.

There's always magic and wonder on Heartbreak Hill. I took photos of the stacked barricades that would soon line Commonwealth Avenue to keep spectators out of the road as the runners made their way to Boylston Street. The photos ignited the excitement of my friends running Boston when I posted them on Facebook. We still felt Johnny Kelley's presence smiling down on us. His photo hangs above our athletic medal display that holds our precious medals from our running adventures.

Next weekend we welcome friends back to Boston and experience all the awe and wonder that is uniquely the Boston Marathon. Today we ran 5 miles on the Hills in Newton and joined with the community of runners counting down to Boston Marathon 2017.

There is a unique energy surrounding the Boston Marathon that you can't help but feel. It includes every runner and every person along the course. It brings every person there together as one. ~Amy Hastings

The Magic of Boston Marathon Weekend   April 17, 2017

How appropriate that the symbol for the Boston Marathon is a unicorn; a magical mythical creature that can never be caught. Yet it is in the act of chasing the Unicorn that we learn nothing is impossible. We can always strive for excellence. There is an enchanted spell that descends on Boston during Boston Marathon weekend. It's a time when everyone talks with everyone else on the MBTA. "You running?" "Where ya from?" "Who won the game?" (referring to the Red Sox playing at Fenway Park). It's a time when you bump into people you haven't seen in awhile and it's as though no time has passed. You hug. You get caught up on each other's lives and then you let them know where you'll be watching the runners on Marathon Monday. Our Boston Marathon weekend adventure began with a stop at the Runners World Pop Up Store across the street from the Expo. Even though we'd only met once in Bermuda, Bart Yasso treated us like dear old friends embracing us in warm hugs.

"My tag line is "Never limit where running can take you," he told us as he signed a copy of his book, "My Life On The Run."

We asked if we could get a photo with him and he said to Tom, "She makes two old guys look good."

As we bid goodbye to attend the Expo, Bart wished us a wonderful race weekend and added, "Hope to see you two soon!"

We returned to the Expo on Saturday afternoon after going on a 5K run around the Reservoir.

"In just about 5 minutes we will be having a moment of silence at 2:49."

The countdown to the moment of silence began with an announcement every minute or so. A hush came over the Hynes Convention Center that made the hair rise on the back of my neck. Tears streamed down my face as Tom and I held hands sharing this moment as One community that is Boston Strong. I was taken aback by my powerful emotional reaction to the moment of silence. I was, for a brief moment, back in time when time stood still four years ago at the Mandarin Oriental Hotel. Celebration quickly turned to chaos and confusion. In the wake of silence, excitement resumed at the Expo.

I noticed that Bermuda Marathon Weekend did not have a booth this year. I emailed Anthony to find out if he was in Boston and that we'd be at the Expo helping out friends at Booth 2828. I didn't hear back from him. We were just about to leave when ....

"Anthony!" Tom yelled.

"You ruined the surprise when you called out my name. I was going to come up from behind and give her a hug!"

We hugged like family hugs each other. With an outstretched arm, Anthony introduced us to his cousin Jo-Ell who was in Boston receiving breast cancer treatment. Although I was not planning on running Bermuda again, and Tom and I were exploring other race destinations for 2018, once you make a friend in Bermuda, they are a friend for life.

Anthony was in town for the Race Directors Training led by Dave McGillivray. He ran the BAA 5K earlier in the day and was going to see the premiere of the "Boston Marathon Documentary" in the evening.

"You know," he said. "I've been thinking about you and thinking about having a walking Marathon in the early Spring in Bermuda. Is that something you might be interested in?"

With eyes lit up, I looked at Tom and said, "What do you think?"

Anthony saw how excited we were at the prospect of the event.

We talked about changes that happened on the Island, and my reasons for not running Bermuda again in 2018. He told us what happened with this year's Race Weekend and steps he was going to take to prevent it from happening again next year.

"We negotiated a great price with the race weekend host hotel. You know the place. The Fairmont Southampton Princess," he told us. "$189 per night."

I flashed back to the after race party we attended at the Princess.

He shared with us that he could not negotiate a rate with The Rosedon. We talked about the changes that were happening at The Rosedon; that was one of the reasons we were not going to return to that property and probably not the Island for awhile.

"What would it take for you to return?"

Tom and I paused ...

"How about if I gave you a complimentary race entry," Anthony offered.

Tom quickly asked, "Could we do an early start?"

"Of course. We just need to work it out with the timing company," Anthony replied.

I smiled coyly.

"What?" Anthony and Tom asked almost at the same time.

"I just went from being 'Easy Out Alper' to receiving an invitational entry to an international race weekend."

"To every kid humiliated by a gym teacher and chosen last for teams, you can still grow up to be a marathon runner like me." ~Mara-Mon

It was a great day when Boston ran again. Tom and I cheered on the runners, gave hugs, gave away one of our fuel belt water bottles that we had for our own hydration and offered lots of cowbell. We stayed at Dean Road and Beacon Street, just shy of mile 22.5 until the back of the pack runners came through. They had to run in very challenging conditions; from high temperatures with sun to a precipitous drop in temperature with clouds and wind. They were delighted we were still out there, cheering them on. We often compare Boston Marathon Weekend to being Christmas in April. There's magic every Boston Marathon Weekend. This is our City and we run Boston!

After agreeing to run the Bermuda Half Marathon in 2018, I had to ask myself again, "What had I just done?" I felt I needed to take a break after running two consecutive half marathons in as many years yet something compelled me to run it again. How do you say no to an invitational race entry? And how do you say no to an invitation from a Bermudian? It was a miracle that I was able to train for and complete those two half marathons after the serious knee injury I suffered in December of 2014. It was time to once again "see what this body can do."

"Life should not be a journey to the grave with the intention of arriving safely in a pretty and well preserved body, but rather to skid in broadside in a cloud of smoke, thoroughly used up, totally worn out, and loudly proclaiming "Wow! What a Ride!" ~Hunter S. Thompson

Michael Aselton 5K Race Report   May 30, 2017

On Friday May 25, 2007, I walked out of the Boston VA Medical Center for the last time. I turned in my ID badge and went through the clearing out process with each department. I came home and sat on my front lawn wondering what had I just done? While I had money in savings after pulling out my entire retirement account from the VA, I had no real plan for the rest of my life. I wasn't even sure that I had 'the rest of my life.' I felt better than I had in years and certainly better than I had in the months leading up the diagnosis of Post-Polio Syndrome. It was a warm, sunny day. I sat in a lawn chair clutching my yet to be published book of poetry, "New World Greetings: Inspirational Poetry and Musings for a New World." I surrendered everything to the Divine.

I kicked off a new decade of healing with - what else - a road race.

We woke up at 5:30 am on Sunday morning. I reminded myself, that there is no such thing as only a 5K. While the distance may be only 3.11 miles, the Great Hyannis Road Race Michael Aselton 5K marked the ushering in of a new decade of healing for me. We did core work on Saturday morning. We picked up our bibs. Paulie was seated in a rocking chair on the porch supervising his staff, and greeting the runners. We walked along Main Street and had lunch at the British Beer Company. We spent the afternoon resting outside near the soon to be opened for the season pool area. This was our first time staying at the Resort in summer. It was a treat to experience the warmer weather amenities.

After core work on Sunday morning, I was inspired to use our in room coffee maker to boil water for our oatmeal. Since gun time was at 7:30 and Starbucks in the hotel lobby didn't open until 6:30, I wanted to make sure that we had enough time to eat at a leisurely pace and get to the starting line without stress. It was a gorgeous day for a race.

Parking was easy. We had plenty of time to stretch our legs before gun time. After a beautiful rendition of the Star Spangled Banner we heard welcoming remarks from a Barnstable Police Officer. He told us how much this race means to the Town of Barnstable. The proceeds benefit the Michael K. Aselton Scholarship Fund and The American Foundation for Suicide Prevention. We stood in the middle of the pack at the starting line and we were off!

Tom checked his Garmin.I was running a sub-16 minute per mile pace which I hadn't done in over a year. The course had spectacular views. Tom checked in with me about the pace.

"Do you have any expectations of the time on the clock for a finish time?"

"I'll be happy if I break 50 minutes," I said. "I've been trying to break that mark for the past year on the treadmill and on tempo runs."

I ran from the inside out being mindful of when I needed to ease up on the throttle of my pace feeling my heart rate soar. We walked and took a water break when my Nike+ announced the miles and stopped at the water stops. A sign of a great race with ideal weather conditions is when you wish the race were longer than a 5K.

Tom happened to catch a glimpse of the finisher's clock as we turned a corner to come into the finish.

"Hey it's 49:14," Tom said.

We kicked it through to the finish line. 49:49! SUCCESS! I broke that once elusive 50-minute mark that had been bugging me for the past year. As always, however, it's not just about the time on the clock but about the time we share together on the roads and what we learn about ourselves as we meet ourselves on the roads.

This race was the first time that I didn't have that trigger fire up from lugging my leg brace. We were last in the back of the pack. It was a "my race, my pace" moment for me enjoying running with Tom by my side. I didn't feel the pressure to speed up and push myself to catch up. I was running at a great pace for me during that first downhill. We caught up with a woman who was coming off of an injury. We both felt proud and honored to be running with each other. After we passed her we came upon a mother with a little girl wearing a t-shirt that said, "We run this town."

As we ran, we chatted about the running club in Connecticut that has children ages 3-12 in it. We talked about the joy of running and marveled at how many children are enjoying the sport at a young age.

We passed them and went on to a very strong finish being cheered on by spectators, volunteers and runners who had already finished the 5K.

We proudly wore our bling as we walked along Main Street to get a proper Sunday breakfast on Cape Cod.

"It was a beautiful day for a race, wasn't it?" one runner asked.

"It certainly was," I said.

"There's no better way to start the day than with a 5K race is there?" he asked.

"Absolutely!" I replied with a smile.

As we sat at a table in the fresh air looking over the menu at "The Egg and I" on Main Street in Hyannis, I felt my heart overflow with gratitude.

What a wonderful way to begin a new decade of healing!

"Thoughts are the language of the brain and feelings are the language of the body. How you think and how you feel creates a state of being." ~Dr. Joe Dispenza

On Believing, Healing and Crushing Goals!   June 22, 2017

From January to late June, my "off season" of training for Bermuda Marathon Weekend, I increased my intensity of cross training and strength training. After working out on the Arc Trainer for a year, I knew it was time to set new goals. My first goal was for .9 mile however long it took me. The next goal was to see if I could hit .9 mile within a 20 minute time limit. I came so close. We increased mileage on the road to Bermuda on Saturday. I knew I had only one more opportunity to open it up and see if I could crush that goal before needing to focus on the mileage to train for Bermuda.

What a contrast to, "If you use it you will lose it. As it is you should prepare to spend the rest of your life in a wheelchair."

On Tuesday, I did not have the intention to set out and crush my goal but something fired up within me. Sweat poured. My heart rate soared. Once I set my intention to crush that goal, I had a single-minded vision and focus. All that mattered in those moments was to see the distance digits change over as I increased my pace. Once I knew I was within striking distance, I garnered more and more momentum in my workout. It took on a life of its own and I hit .9 before the 20 minute mark. I kept pumping away until I hit the 20 minute time limit. As my heart rate slowed down while I stretched, I smiled to myself with a Cheshire cat grin of satisfaction.

I'm ready to take on 5.5 miles on Saturday on the road to my third consecutive Bermuda Half Marathon. It will be a first for me. It's time to take another leap of faith for that's what believing, healing and crushing goals is all about.

"The body believes what the mind can conceive." ~Bernie Siegel, MD

Training officially began today for Team McManus on the road to Bermuda Half Marathon 2018. I'm in uncharted territory. As I lay in bed this morning, preparing for my first training run with meditation, the thought, "Your body remembers how to train for and run a half marathon," floated through my mind.

When I first set out on my quest to heal my life, I wrote a line in a poem, "The body remembers what the mind forgets....until it's time to heal."

Throughout my healing journey, I have resurrected and healed traumatic memories while also reaching back into the recesses of my mind to resurrect positive memories from before polio and trauma. I was a graceful ballerina. I was strong and flexible. One morning, as I put my feet on the wooden floor in our bedroom, I felt the energy surge and remembered what it was like to be in ballet class before tragedy struck my life.

After writing the poem, "Running the Race,", I watched the "Run Forrest Run" scene from Forrest Gump over and over again. Dr. Joe Dispenza talks about the power of mirror neurons. By observing someone else performing an action our body responds as if we were performing that action. Immersing myself in the sport of running allowed my body to heal from the effects of paralytic polio. I provide a healing environment for mind, body and soul with my 5 day training cycle. After my meditation, I was ready to get out for our training run.

The weather called for rain but the temperature was 77 degrees. It was cloudy as we had our breakfast, did our core work and stretched. By the time the water bottles were filled and water belts were packed, the mist turned to a steady rainfall. Instead of our original plan to run around Jamaica Pond, we headed out to a part of the Boston Marathon course on Beacon Street. We could always head into a building for cover and the buildings would provide a buffer for the wind and rain.

Tom and I embraced the challenge of the run with uphills and downhills, rain, humidity and moments of sunshine breaking through the clouds. We ignited the passion of being endurance runners again and imagined what it's going to be like to once again run the Bermuda Half Marathon together. We took 11 seconds per mile off of our pace from last week, ran hills and added .5 miles to the run. It's all coming back to me now - because the body remembers!

Born to Run

Born free
born to run
run free
unencumbered untethered unshackled
pouring energy into my running form
liquid gold once fired in the crucible
now my treasure born of my Spirit molded with alchemy
refining
my precious treasure once buried
the map safely tucked away
X marks the spot
a new starting line.

Poised and ready
to go the distance
all out without hesitation
all is healed at last
my pace swift
Mercury and Hermes pace me on winged feet
I AM
born to run
running free
joyfully crossing the finish line with ease.

"*Most people never run far enough on their first wind to find out they have a second wind.*" ~William James

On Finding a Second Wind   July 3, 2017

I knew it was going to be a hard run with the forecast for heat and humidity. Even with a morning run, and running on a relatively flat course along Boston Harbor, it was a challenging run. During one stretch of the run, the sun was beating down on us with the heat rising off of the asphalt. All I could think about was going into the ocean for an ice bath after the run. I experienced uncomfortable sensations of a challenging run while knowing these are the runs that prepare me for race day. We were mindful to take extra water stops, and we slowed down our pace. Tom and I joked how on some runs we feel like we could go on forever but on this run, "not so much." We could feel ourselves slogging through the run and then, after mile 3.5 we got our second wind.

163

Nothing shifted around us but something shifted within us as we shifted our focus from feeling hot and sluggish to looking out on the water visualizing the Bermuda Half Marathon. After we got our second wind, we felt as though we could run for miles. We refueled with delicious hearty, healthy sandwiches from American Provisions in South Boston and recovered by diving into the refreshing ice cold waters of the Atlantic Ocean.

6.5 Mile(stone) and a Visit with the Race Director   July 24, 2017

Team McManus is feeling the momentum of being on the road to the Bermuda Half Marathon 2018. Although it was another hot steamy Saturday as we ran along Boston Harbor from Castle Island to U. Mass. Boston, we hit a training milestone. We once again made sure we dialed back our pace, hydrated and fueled keeping our eyes on the prize.

An older runner passed us, also dripping with sweat.

"Great job guys," he nodded. "Keep it up."

"You too!" we said in unison.

We sought out shade whenever we could along the course and I imagined immersing myself in an ice bath once we'd get home. It held me in good stead as we wound our way through the paths by picturesque Boston Harbor. As many played volleyball or tanned themselves on the beach, Tom and I kept a steady pace. We felt triumphant when we heard Nike+ say "Congratulations! You've reached your goal of 6.5 miles."

Clarence and Anthony were coming to Boston for Dave McGillivray's Sports Classic Weekend Expo. We planned to meet them for dinner at Salvatore's Restaurant in the Merrimack Valley near their hotel.

"There was a serious accident on our way from New York," Clarence told me on the phone.

"We're fine and there were no fatalities but we will arrive too late for dinner. We are going to head directly to our hotel."

Disappointed, we went ahead and had our post run dinner at Salvatore's where we dined overlooking the Merrimack River. We were treated to a glorious sunset and delicious Italian food. Anthony and Clarence were planning to leave after the Expo and races on Sunday. We resigned ourselves to the fact that it wasn't meant to be to get together this trip. Anthony was planning another trip to Boston to see us.

Clarence and Anthony called us late Saturday; they would finish at the Expo at 11 on Sunday.

"We'll come to you," Clarence said.

I was excited to be able to reciprocate the hospitality to Anthony and Clarence we experienced from them while we were in Bermuda.

"Anthony says he knows where Brookline is."

They called at around 11:30 and said they were leaving Andover (about an hour and change drive away from where we live).

"Would you like to come for lunch?" I asked.

"Well that will need to happen love," Clarence replied.

Tom and I rummaged through the fridge to see what we could put together for a luncheon. While I set up the outside table, Tom went to Star Market down the street from where we live. We made a luscious buffet spread on our indoor dining room table. With a wonderful array of food, we had sparkling conversation under the sprawling tree in our yard.

Anthony remarked, "It's such a treat to sit under a big tree. And I love your neighborhood. As you know we have nothing like this in Bermuda."

We talked about the great time they had at the Race Expo.

"Looks like we've got quite the group of Bostonians getting ready to come run in Bermuda this year," Anthony beamed.

"I'm so happy for you especially after what happened last year. It's going to be epic," I said with a broad smile.

We laughed and shared stories about our relationship with Bermuda. I proudly showed photos and memorabilia from our many trips to the Island. What a delight to walk down memory lane with Bermudians.

"Be sure to help me spread the word that any of you who arrive on Thursday I want you to join us for the kickoff party for Race Weekend. We're back at Bacardi Headquarters this year."

"Of course we will! And you know I'll be working my social media mojo again."

After a brief lull in our conversation ...

"So let me ask you....is there a time limit on the Half? Do we need an early start?"

In true Bermudian style, Anthony and Clarence gave us a rather lengthy detailed explanation about why they had to put forth a time limit on the Half Marathon along with anecdotes from previous years' race experiences.

"Having said all of that", Anthony said, "As long as you get in before my last marathoner crosses the finish line, you'll be fine."

"We figure we will finish in just under four hours," I said.

With a warm Bermudian smile Clarence said, "Oh my you'll be fine!"

We talked about the rest of their trip Stateside and about the unique design of the medals this year. They swore us to secrecy after they described the intricate medal design for this year's weekend races.

We had a long goodbye as they regaled us with more insider stories from the America's cup and lots of hugs, joy and laughter.

We sent them off by saying, "See you in Bermuda!"

On Ten Miles, Turkey Hot Dogs, Ponchos and Running Camaraderie
October 1, 2017

I knew there was a good chance of rain for our 10 mile run yesterday. Tom and I got up early hoping that we would be able to beat the rain. We saw patches of blue sky and were cautiously optimistic. Tom skillfully rolled up the ponchos I purchased on a whim at Target a few weeks ago when I had to pick up a few other items. The first mile was without rain and then there were slow plops of raindrops. The great debate - should we bring out the ponchos now or wait and see what happens. Given the foreboding sky, we put them on. As a runner passed, she smiled and laughed at us wearing ponchos when there were only a few raindrops falling on the gravel path around the Reservoir.

"She laughed at me," I said out loud.

The rain picked up to a steady pace. "What a blessing you thought to purchase these ponchos," Tom said. "They sure beat the trash bags we used to use."

We saw a few runner friends and stopped for a moment to chat. We got caught up on the latest happenings in our lives and on the roads. We acknowledged what dedicated runners we were to be out training in the rain.

Since we were running 3 times around the Reservoir, we had the opportunity to pass the same runners a few times; including the one who "laughed" at me. She smiled as we passed her as if to say, "Yeah you were right." Another runner waved heartily as she braved the elements in a tank top and capris.

A neighbor running with her dog passed by us.

With a hint of sarcasm in her voice she said, "Enjoy." Her dog shook off the rain and continued running with joy and reckless abandon.

"I'm taking my lead from your dog," I said.

"We should all have that attitude," she said.

Unlike many who may experience running in the rain a nuisance. I feel deeply blessed and grateful I am to be able to run in the rain, navigating, sometimes without success, the mud puddles. As a survivor of paralytic polio, lugging a full metal leg brace and then not having the flexibility or freedom in my body as I got older, I never had the chance to splash in puddles and run in the rain. Shortly after being diagnosed with Post-Polio Syndrome, I had a dream about splashing in the puddles without my leg brace. Imagine the scene with Gene Kelly singing and dancing to the title song from "Singing in the Rain." That dream inspired this poem:

Come Out and Play
Arms flung open wide dancing in the rain
pure abiding joy to feel alive again
healing tears fall and blend in God's puddle
no time to sit in a corner and huddle
all the old rules driven by fears
washed away now by God's loving tears
the imprint dad left no longer remains
rain washes away all of the stains
baptized with love, Truth lights my way
the sun shines through on this rainy day
splashing and laughing my heart opens wide
embracing and flowing I'm one with the tide
God takes my hand release the old way
bathe in my glory come out and play.

I joyfully ran in the rain without a leg brace training for my third half marathon in as many years. We made a quick pit stop at home to fill up water bottles, use the bathroom and we got on our way for the final miles on our double digit training run. While waiting for the light to change, standing on the corner of Route 9, Paula rolled down her window and honked at us. We waved and smiled. What an energy boost! After our run, I thanked her on Facebook for the honk. She said how inspired she feels whenever she sees our post run photos. Twice around the Route 9 Reservoir, up the hills back to our house, the last mile up and down Eliot Street finishing strong with another hill and we deposited another 10 miles in the Bank of Bermuda. Double digits - done!

I felt the gravel from the path around the Reservoir hit the back of my legs. Our running shoes squished as we ran. We were of one mind and one purpose; to finish 10 miles. I felt our pace quicken as we got closer to the end of the run. I recalled what our personal trainer told us during our 2009 Boston Marathon training. Once you're on the back half of the miles you need to run, you can begin to pick up the pace. One more mile to go as we passed our home; an out and back .5 of a mile. The rain tapered off and by the end of the run the rain had stopped. We were soaked to the skin and muddy yet felt ebullient and accomplished.

I have often compared training for an endurance event to being pregnant. You experience craving for foods, you have sensations in your body that accompany intense training, and most importantly of all, after the event is over, you swear you're never going to do another one. You forget all about the pain and do it all over again. I woke up sore this morning moving gingerly until I could get everything in motion with our core work exercises to begin the day. I was grateful for the warm pool at Boston Sports Club to continue to gain momentum in training and bring ease to the aches and pains from a 10 mile run in the rain. I reminded myself that sore = strong. But I digress....

Last week I craved hot dogs but knowing hot dogs are not exactly a nutritious and healthy choice, we decided turkey hot dogs would be a great compromise. Tom took off his rain soaked poncho and fired up the grill. We relished our two turkey dogs. While I could have easily devoured macaroni salad and potato salad for sides, we went with a healthy option of a salad followed by a chocolate smoothie. I was chilled and damp from the run but knew I had to muster my courage to get into an ice bath with Epsom salts to recover. I lowered myself into the icy waters wearing a hat, a hoodie and having my iPhone handy to go through my Facebook stream. I visualized how good a warm shower was going to feel after my ice bath. A year ago, it rained and was windy on the day of our 9 mile run. We opted to go indoors and did 6 miles on the treadmill and 3 miles on the bike. This year we are training ourselves mind, body and soul to have the best race day possible on January 14th, 2018.

Countdown to Bermuda: On Faith and Determination October 5, 2017

According to the website's countdown clock, it's 99 days until the kickoff of Bermuda Marathon Weekend. Another week of training is in the books for Team McManus.

Tuesdays are my cross training days at the gym to match Tom's Tuesday morning runs. As I was walking to the gym, everything seemed to ache. Since our 10 mile run in the rain, I had intermittent back spasms, and a lot of joint pain. I used techniques that I learned from Dr. Candace Pert and Dr. Joe Dispenza. I discovered their work from watching the movie "What the bleep do we know."

"I created this I can uncreate it. This pain isn't an indication that something is wrong with me. My body recovers well and with ease from any challenge I put it through. I am healthy, healed, whole and strong."

I felt fear surge through me and it momentarily took over the power of the affirmations. I know I've already healed, but training for another endurance event brings new powerful sensations. Training for another half marathon challenges me to have my voice and faith be louder than what I was told by doctors and physical therapists through the years. It takes strength and courage to trust in my body and reverse the thoughts and feelings that were a result of having been conditioned to the effects of polio and trauma. I bring compassion and Divine healing to the fear. One painful step at a time I walked to Boston Sports Club. As I entered the Club with people pouring sweat, pounding out miles on the treadmill, lifting weights, riding the bike and experiencing the energy of dedication to their health and wellness journey, I came out of the locker room with a powerful resolve. I thought greater than my circumstances. I remembered the skilled and loving touch of Dr. Ryan, who reminded me to set goals not limits. I imagined him taping my left knee and calf as he had done in New York in November during one of his visits to the States from China. I felt his healing presence with me reminding me that I have the power to heal.

I plugged in my headphones and got into the rhythm of the Arc Trainer and then the Bike. To my surprise, after my 50 minute workout was done, I had gone 6.4 miles which was the farthest I had gone during my cardio workouts. It helps to keep a training journal. As I walked back to my car the pain was gone! (Aah the power of endorphins.) Anytime that I begin to doubt that my body is healed (regardless how appearances may seem) I look at the scar on my nose. For many years it would bleed, crust over and reopen. Many said that I needed to go to a doctor but I had faith and patience. It took 3 years. What was once an angry looking wound, is now merely a scar. It is a constant reminder of my body's capacity to heal when I tap into the Divine intelligence within me and around me.

The mind/body connection is more powerful than we were ever led to believe. We were led to believe that doctors know best, better safe than sorry and to mind what *they* were telling us. There is a time and place for Western medicine otherwise I would have a crooked left leg and not be able to move my arm when a staph infection invaded my shoulder joint, but there are many doctors who hand down edicts ignoring our body's innate capacity to heal. To better understand how powerful our thoughts are, I want you to think about what happens when you see a photo of delicious food. Do you feel your mouth water? That's because our mind is anticipating how that food will taste triggering a cascade of chemical reactions in our body. Our body can't distinguish between actually tasting the food and our minds thinking about tasting the food. Our body responds to our thoughts. To repeat the quote from Billy Mills as he created the biggest upset in Olympic history: *"The subconscious mind cannot tell the difference between imagination and reality."*

I don't have time for a relapse of symptoms or to move backwards in my healing journey. I found my way to a new chiropractor in Boston who is partnering with me on this leg of my healing journey. After my treatment with her, I felt the wonderful effects of wholesome healing through her gentle, low force method of chiropractic care. Whenever I even think about easing up on my training, I think about how far I've come on my quest to heal my life. I think about my village. Their love fuels me on the roads and in my life. They uphold and uplift me along with my deep abiding Faith. Two days of rest and recovery are on tap before depositing another 10 miles in the Bank of Bermuda. The countdown has begun. We are ahead in mileage from our training plans in the last two years. My plan is to keep practicing and rehearsing, conditioning my body to my new mind healed from the effects of polio and trauma, feeling the joy in the journey and allowing the love that surrounds from my village to propel me forward on this amazing marathon of life.

A Perfect 10 for 10.5 - I've Got This   October 22, 2017

In our training plan, I amped up the mileage early to try to ensure that we'd be able to get in quality miles for a good percentage of our outdoor long runs. Last year we went indoors early in the training and toughed out miles in less than optimal weather conditions. Yesterday was a gift from the weather gods. The weather was what we'd expect to experience in Bermuda but certainly a surprise for October 21st in Boston. I experienced race day conditions with a 10.5 mile training run wearing shorts and a tank top. Last year I overdressed on race day which was definitely a factor in muscle spasms and cramps at mile 10. After two 10 mile training runs, I broke through the psychological barrier of what happened to me last year. I have focus and intention that melt fears. Dr. Joe's work with new daily meditations help me experience confidence and strength in my ability to go the distance for the 3rd consecutive year. I am taking healing to a new level.

Tom and I simulated fueling, hydration and pacing for race day. I visualized our day and I've let go of a finishing time. (Are you saying to yourself, "Well it's about time Mary?")

What a blessing to have Anthony's reassurance this year about no time limit for this runner girl. I hear the sweet refrain echo in my thoughts, "As long as you finish before my last marathoner, you'll be just fine!"

After yesterday's training run, I felt "I've got this." We've done a few long runs in rain, a few in chilly weather and yesterday we ran in absolutely beautiful perfect weather conditions. As the miles added up, the doubts and fears mounted up. To counter them, I engaged in positive self-talk, journaling about my fears so I can be aware of them and release them. I feel deep in my soul I am meant to go the distance once again. Only 2.5 miles left to finish a half marathon. I've got this - especially after a perfect 10 kind of day.

Countdown to Bermuda: How Lucky Could We Get?
November 26, 2017

Sunny and temperatures in the 50's on November 25th in New England. A few moments of headwind but overall it was another gift from the running gods for perfect running weather. Before we went on our 11.5 mile run, I set my intention for our run. I found this quote that captured my heart and soul:

"Running is just such a monastery- a retreat, a place to commune with God and yourself, a place for psychological and spiritual renewal."
~George A. Sheehan

Tom and I often joke that we belong to the church of the long run. Going out on a long run on a picture perfect day in Boston, unplugged with Tom by my side is a treat and a retreat. We had the route well planned out. We arrived at the Cleveland Circle Reservoir. Tom was going to park where we parked two weeks ago for our 11 mile run in freezing temps. I did not want to recall the run where I wanted to quit after 6 miles. I was miserable for the last 5 miles struggling with every step. Once I saw our car, the finish line was in sight. My energy picked up and all thoughts of being frozen melted away. It was our toughest training run of the season; one that I didn't need to remember by parking in the same spot along the top of the Reservoir.

"Hey Tom. Why don't we park on Beacon Street at the foot of the Reservoir where we parked for our last run when we trained for Bermuda 2016?"

"Great idea," he replied.

We did 2 loops around the Chestnut Hill Reservoir and then ran 3 loops around the Route 9 Reservoir near our house. We kept marveling at how warm the sun felt. We focused on our mental preparation for race weekend.

We returned to the Reservoir to finish our miles.

Our fueling and hydration plan is set and held us in good stead through the 11.5 miles. I reflected on the miracle of healing that I've been able to co-create with the Divine during these past 10 years. I felt the presence of the Divine blessing us as we train mind, body and soul. I'm running unencumbered and free tethered only to the Divine. I feel the excitement building and felt a gush of gratitude to realize how close we are to the starting line of my third consecutive Bermuda Half Marathon. How lucky can you get?

Soon after that training run, my body began to experience the toll of training for a third half marathon in as many years. Painful back spasms plagued me and my right hip and groin were inflamed. My chiropractor brought healing to my weary and painful body as we added on the miles. I knew I was not going to quit, but, I did know that after our 12 mile run, the hay was in the barn and I did not need to do another 12 or a 12.5 mile run. I knew that the rest and long taper time would be more beneficial for me on race day.

After Saturday's run, and with the extended weather forecast of cold temperatures with the chance of snow coming our way I knew that we hit the peak of training. I was wise preparing for the whims of Mother Nature in Boston. By building miles quickly early on in our training, I knew we'd have the flexibility to either go indoors or taper miles as we moved into December. As my body experienced the aches and pains of going the distance, it was a judicious plan.

The original route for Saturday's training run was to drive to the Cleveland Circle Reservoir, run once around the Rezzie as we like to call it, head down Beacon Street (along the Boston Marathon route) to Coolidge Corner and back, to the "small" Reservoir on Route 9, 3 times around the small Reservoir and back to Cleveland Circle. When I came out of Saturday morning's meditation, I knew we needed to make it a dress rehearsal for race day and change the route!

"I think we've gone around the Reservoirs one too many times for our long runs," I declared.

We packed our gear with hydration and fueling as if it were race day. Of course our attire could not be what it was going to be on race day since it was 37 degrees. Race day in Bermuda should be in the high 60's and low 70's with a mixture of sun and clouds. We were blessed with a dry day without any wind. I was amazed how easily we negotiated the hills along Beacon Street; especially the last steep hill as we headed into Kenmore Square. We needed a pit stop and went into Hotel Commonwealth. It was all decked out for the holidays. Christmas and 2018 were right around the corner. We ran down Commonwealth Avenue and took a right on Hereford and left on Boylston. Boylston Street was busy with pedestrians. It was too difficult to dodge them and keep a steady pace. We weaved our way through the crowds on Boylston Street until we could cross over to the Commonwealth Avenue Mall. On the Mall and into the Public Gardens, the holiday atmosphere of lights draping the bushes and the hustle and bustle of holiday shoppers was in high gear. Bermuda Marathon Weekend was on the horizon. I imagined the remnants of holiday decorations on Front Street waiting for our return to Bermuda.

As we headed back to Cleveland Circle, the clouds moved in and the day got chilly but our Spirits were high. I had to make another pit stop (cold weather and being an older woman does that you know). I thought I could wait until we got to Marathon Sports farther down Beacon Street. As we approached the Holiday Inn several blocks and hills before Marathon Sports, I realized I was not going to make it. I'd gone to Rotary Club meetings at the Hotel sharing my journey as a polio survivor and supporting the End Polio Now campaign. I remembered the restrooms were down the stairs off of an entrance on Beacon Street. "Restrooms are for hotel guests only" the sign said as we entered. Tom ran down the stairs and did a quick surveillance. Singing the Mission Impossible theme song, Tom gave me the all clear. On the way back to Cleveland Circle we navigated the hills with surprising ease. I stopped only once in the middle of the steep hill at mile 8.

We returned to the car to calculate the home stretch of our 12 mile run.

Once around the Rezzie and a short down and back from the car and we'd be done.

The official countdown to Bermuda Marathon Weekend is on. My body is ready for taper time.

The Universe Has My Back   January 5, 2018

We know that taper time can wreak havoc with one's mental status. The downshifting of energy to allow the body to recover and have lots in the tank on race day is a crucial time but, that's when the mind can run amuck. After a track and treadmill run last Saturday and a few treadmill runs since our last long run, my lower back felt tight; the soreness in my right hip worsened. I had a great session with my chiropractor on Wednesday that helped ease the pain. In addition to the strain I put on my body training for a third half marathon in as many years, there was a powerful mental component to the pain. Tom listened with compassion as I shared my fears, tears and doubts about going the 13.1 distance again. I felt tired, sore and insecure. I wanted to just sit on the beach. But how could I possibly miss the excitement and adventure of race day? How could I possibly settle for a life any less than the magnificent life I am meant to live? How could I not shine and how could I rob myself of our victory lap. By the time my last forkful of salmon was consumed, I was fired up and very excited for Bermuda Marathon Weekend 2018.

We had a wonderful meditation and I had a wonderful night's sleep.

I felt energized this morning and despite some lingering back pain and hip soreness I know I am going to be great on race day. Running is my therapy and my medicine. I feel better when I run and I forget about all the aches and pains in my body because I am focused on the beautiful world outside of myself. My body heals when I run outdoors. That's the irony of taper time. It's a time to recover and heal and is vital to the training process, but I lose out on the benefits of running.

I had the most remarkable experience while in the shower this morning. I was in the present moment feeling blessed and baptized by the hot water. I knew in every fiber of my Being healing has happened. I am poised and ready to go the distance.

I felt the presence of Dr. Moskowitz.

I learned he was a physician ahead of his time when I found this article in the New York Times:

The Westchester Post-Polio Group is grateful to Dr. Eugene Moskowitz (Letters to the Editor, March 3) for providing the public with a concrete demonstration of the negative and patronizing attitude many of us encountered from physicians. If Dr. Moskowitz finds "no reason to suspect deterioration in the nerve cells in the spinal cords," we suggest that he read "Proceedings From the First Annual Symposium on the Late Effects of Poliomyelitis," in which highly respected members of his own profession advance excellent medical arguments and research reports in support of exactly that theory.

Here is what my beloved Dr. Moskowitz wrote:

Caution and Hope On Polio 'Signs'
Published: March 3, 1985
I read with interest the article entitled "A Group for Polio Survivors Who Have New Symptoms" (Feb. 10).

Having supervised the rehabilitation of poliomyelitis patients at Grasslands Hospital during the epidemics of the 50's and 60's, probably including the "then" infants mentioned in the article, I would like to add a word of caution and even hope as an afterthought.

Firstly, there is no reason to suspect deterioration in the nerve cells in the spinal cord. After 30 years, one must accept some loss of endurance, increased fatigue and even some discomfort induced by other unrelated medical problems. This is true in the athlete with repeated injuries, in the obese person with back problems and even in the jogger with foot ailments.

Any individual with paralytic disability in an extremity will experience the normal process of "wear and tear" except that it may be more difficult to adjust to it. Just as one learned to compensate for the initial impairment so must one adjust to the later, more subtle changes rather than develop an emotional hang up of being a "polio victim." ~EUGENE MOSKOWITZ, M.D. Mount Vernon

During my rehabilitation, he would have me bend over and touch my toes. He ran his healing hand along my spinal cord and across my lower back. That memory lit up my entire body and being. When I got out of the shower I bent over and touched my toes and felt a surge of his healing energy go through me. I am going for the Gold Medal of healing. Shortly after my diagnosis, I couldn't even stand up from a chair without putting my hands on a table or the sink in the bathroom for support. My goal now is to stand up and be pain free, and free in mind, body and soul.

Spirit is speaking to me, "Don't worry about the muscle spasms or the hip. I've got your back and you've got your race."

Mental Preparation   **January 6-10, 2018**

During this morning's meditation I saw myself out on the course happy, laughing and dancing. My pain and spasms are illusions and I'm making up my mind to feel healthy, happy and whole in my body. The time is now! It's not about the moment to moment sensations but overcoming myself and my past, feeling whole. There were lingering doubts about my ability to go the distance again and that I belong among the community of international runners. The Universe responded with an email from Anthony with an attachment that contained a gold leaf invitation to attend the Sponsor's Cocktail Reception at Bacardi's. I took out the Course Map and marked it with our fueling and hydration plan. I closed my eyes and visualized race day remembering how awesome I felt when I ran the Bermuda Half Marathon in 2016.

I exchanged telephone numbers with friends who are returning for Race Weekend. I channeled my nervous energy into packing, checking off items on my to do list and imagining how incredible the warm weather was going to feel in the wake of our recent Blizzard of 2018. I was surprisingly calm about the weather which had paralyzed the Northeast and cancelled flights. I knew in every fiber of my being that I was meant to go the distance for the third time.

As I felt the muscle spasms and the pain in my hip, and groin, I had fleeting thoughts of wanting to go to Bermuda to relax and enjoy a vacation.

I'd respond to those fleeting thoughts with, "Why am I going to miss out on all the fun. I don't have to worry about pace or my time."

Before leaving for Bermuda, I saw my chiropractor for a last minute tune up. She told me I had a significant muscle strain, but knew how important this race was for me. She blessed me in going the distance citing how this time of rest and the adjustments would hold me in good stead. I reminded myself that all sensations pass and elevated emotions stimulate healing. My meditations became more powerful than my doubts and fears. I set the intention to have fun, finish and celebrate my miracle of healing. During my meditations, I exposed the roots of fear. I dug them up and planted new seeds of possibility to take root. I went over the course map and imagined every mile of the beautiful Half Marathon course feeling the pain drain out of my hip and beautiful nourishment healing my spinal cord. In my mind's eye, I created a perfect race day. I reminded myself of all the fabulous Facebook posts and well wishes I received. I reminded myself of my purpose: to inspire others with my courage, my strength and my willingness to go the distance.

There were clear skies and no storms in the forecast. Our bags were packed. Our passports were safely tucked away in my pocketbook and we were once again granted a TSA pre-check after I checked in for our flights on line. Our wonderful running friend Amy graciously agreed to take care of our cat Jamie while we were gone. She had the keys and the instructions for food, water and TLC; her two children were very excited to have the opportunity to care for a cat. They instantly fell in love with Jamie and the feeling was mutual. Jamie is usually a very shy cat who will run into the dormer when anyone comes into the house. She lay on the bed while Amy's children petted her. All signs were pointing to a magical and memorable trip for Bermuda Race Weekend.

We departed in the early morning for Boston's Logan International Airport treating ourselves to limo service. The driver arrived early and helped us with our bags. The weather was a balmy 34 degrees after a stretch of bitter cold snowy days. We prepared to board our Delta flight while the sun rose over Boston. We met a few runner friends at the gate for our flight and enjoyed Facebook banter with our friends at the Jet Blue terminal. After a smooth and quick flight, we left Boston and winter behind us. Walking down the stairs to the tarmac, I breathed in the fragrant Bermuda air and allowed the sense of adventure to fill me. While we waited in line to have our passport stamped and to be welcomed back to Bermuda, we saw our friends from the Jet Blue flight and runners we met during last year's race weekend. I marvel at how we can meet a runner once, reconnect after a year as though no time had passed and feel like old friends.

We collected our luggage, and since we had nothing to declare in Customs, quickly exited the terminal. We were greeted by the driver from the transportation service arranged by the Fairmont. Much to our surprise and delight Anthony was waiting for the flights from Boston.

"You promised me there would be no snow in Bermuda," I said as Anthony and I exchanged a warm hug. He was dressed in Bermuda shorts and a t-shirt.

With a hearty laugh and a wink he said, "Oh would you like me to bring some in so that you'll feel right at home? I'd been watching what your weather had been doing."

He came to pick up the special awards personally delivered by Dick Ashworth, Owner of Ashworth Awards who designed the special bling for race weekend. Dick, his wife Kim and their two daughters came for the weekend. On our way to the hotel, I asked Dick if Anthony ordered enough medals for all the finishers this year. Dick said that he ordered at least 1,000 medals and they all arrived safe and sound. Our driver gave us a guided tour of the South Shore en route to our hotel. He made a few stops and asked if we'd like to get out and take photos; Bermudian hospitality at its finest.

At check in we were asked by the Front Desk staff if we wanted to upgrade our room to an Ocean View. We declined the offer; a decision prompted by the Divine.

The first order of business was food. After all we were running 13.1 miles in a few days. We only had a few snacks on the plane after a very early morning breakfast. It was 2:30 pm Bermuda time. We ate outside overlooking palm trees, the hotel pool and accompanied by the songs of Bermuda birds at the Jasmine Lounge. I had a sumptuous Crispy Fried Snapper sandwich with Pineapple Slaw. Tom savored the Rooster Wooster sandwich: Fried Chicken and Pickled Red Onions. Sparkling water with a twist of lemon tickled our taste buds. We took a collective sigh of relief that we made it through training and could now relax and enjoy the time leading up to race day. As we bantered back and forth about whether or not we were going to go on a shake out run, I realized that I needed to rest and allow my body to be in the best possible shape for Sunday.

It was time to transform from Bostonians and trade our winter attire for beach clothes. We boarded the shuttle to the Fairmont's private beach. Tom and I walked along the pink sand. The turquoise blue water swirled around me encouraging an incredible lightness of Being. We kept an eye on the time to make sure we'd have enough time to shower and change for our evening in Hamilton.

As the cab pulled up to the Bacardi Headquarters, we saw everyone gathered on the outside patio for the kick off to Bermuda Marathon Weekend. There was an open bar and appetizers being passed around while announcements and introductions were made. After the formal program, Tom and I strolled down Front Street to The Pickled Onion. There was a gentle breeze and we wore a short sleeve shirt and a sweater. What a blessing to escape the New England winter in the middle of January. We were going to meet a very special person and her "running wife" for dinner.

We hadn't planned on going into Hamilton on Thursday but once we received the invitation to the reception shortly before we left for our trip, we knew we had to change our plans. On a whim I messaged Denise McMillan to see if she wanted to meet up for dinner. When she let me know she was returning to Bermuda for this year's race weekend, I let out a screech that could have been heard from Boston to Kentucky. I suggested we meet for dinner at The Pickled Onion after the reception. Denise and her "running wife" Lanette were staying in Hamilton.

After we ordered, Denise shared the story of how she found me via Instagram even though I wasn't active on Instagram on the eve of the 2016 Bermuda Half Marathon. While occasionally glancing up to take in the scene of the beautiful Bermuda Harbor, Denise became animated.
"There I was looking for the hashtag runbermuda."

She inserted her own music while tapping her fingers on the table.

"What were the chances that our numbers would be in sequence? I 'followed you to Facebook' and when I read your story I was moved to tears. I prayed for your health that night and knew I **had** to find you the next morning."

I was enthralled to hear her recount the story without the filter of pre-race jitters. After Denise shared the story and before our dinner arrived, amidst laughter and joy in awe of what brought us together, Denise went into her bag.

She presented me with a box. "Never bought, only given." Inside was a terrycloth sweat wristband engraved with one word, "INSPIRE."

As she told me the story of how she submitted my story to Run the Bluegrass to get the wristband to bring with her to Bermuda, the tears streamed down my face. I was a puddle of tears of joy and gratitude. I joked that they should move the bread out of the way before I made it soggy.

BECAUSE

"*I met Mary on a plane from Boston to Bermuda in 2016. She overcame unspeakable trauma as a young girl, post polio syndrome as an adult and yet trained to run the Boston Marathon as a mobility impaired runner. She is now training for her 3rd Bermuda Half Marathon. She blogs about running, volunteers for local Boston races and I plan on seeing her again in Jan. 2018 in Bermuda as we both tackle that race. I recently bought her a RTB {Run the Bluegrass} shirt to take to her. She's truly an inspiration to anyone that is lucky enough to cross her path.*"

Denise went on to say that she hoped one day we would come to Kentucky to Run The Bluegrass and she would host us. She brought us Run The Bluegrass T shirts and a coffee mug.

181

Hours passed as we dined on delicious food, laughed and talked about all things running and life. Despite being up since 4:30 am to travel, we were all energized by the love, the gratitude and the inspiration that was the weave of the tapestry that created strong bonds for us as running family.

We said good night, wished them well in their first two legs of the Challenge, and that we'd see each other on Sunday morning before the Half.

A Sign and Bib Pick Up   January 12, 2018

No alarms were set for Friday morning and it felt wonderful to sleep in and awaken to a Bermudaful day.

We opened the door to our balcony to see palm trees and hear Bermuda bird songs. We went to Windows on the Sound restaurant for breakfast where floor to ceiling windows overlook the ocean. I wanted to stick to my pre-race fueling plan breakfast of oatmeal, banana, juice and toast. We brought our own packets of oatmeal and the breakfast buffet supplied the rest. However, I could not resist the melt in your mouth poppy seed muffins. After all, I was on vacation and you only live once. We read the Royal Gazette while savoring our breakfast. I placed my spoon down on the table and paused from looking at the newspaper. I reminisced with Tom about our dear friend Herb. With a jolt, I was drawn to look outside. I noticed the contrast of the sun and the mist coming off of the ocean. It was as though time stood still. My gaze was drawn to look up. There was a rainbow. I cried tears of joy and gratitude.

"Are you okay?" the woman at the next table asked us.

"It's a sign from a friend of ours who introduced us to Bermuda," I said without concern for what this total stranger might think of my declaration.

"Oh I totally believe in signs," she said.

We chatted for a few moments and they wished us a wonderful weekend.

I knew it was Herb saying hello to us blessing our weekend. Despite back and hip pain everything was going to be just fine. Right after I took a photo of the rainbow, it disappeared.

Sporting a Bermuda Marathon Weekend 2017 t-shirt in the elevator, a woman with a long blond braid said to me, "It's nice to see somebody wearing that t-shirt."

"What do you mean?" I asked.

"I sell Bermuda Marathon Weekend t-shirts and wrist bracelets at the Expo," she said.

"I'm Susan."

"I'm Mary McManus. Wait are you Anthony's girlfriend?"

"Yes…I know about you. I recognized the shaking."

She was referring to my head tremors and then caught herself.

"Don't worry about it Susan. I'm so happy to meet you and I'm delighted Anthony shares my story."

We walked and talked from the elevator to the front lobby. She was in a hurry because she had work to do for the weekend. We had work to do mentally preparing ourselves for race day.

We spent the morning relaxing on the beach with gentle walks along the soft pink sand. We went for a swim in the afternoon to stay loose before boarding the shuttle bus into Hamilton to pick up our bibs and get provisions at Miles Market. The hotel did not serve breakfast before 7:00 am and we wanted to make sure we had everything we'd need to fuel for race day. The excitement was infectious on the shuttle ride into Hamilton. We were treated to a breathtaking Bermuda sunset as we left the resort. The energy was electric at the Expo and Bib pick up. We saw runner friends that we'd met in Bermuda, and runner friends from the States. Tony Bean, the official photographer for Race Weekend warmly greeted us and took photos of Team McManus.

We walked the short distance to Miles Market where we bought bananas, bagels, granola and oranges. It was a thrill to be back feeling like Bermuda was our second home. We passed runners with their bibs on for the Front Street Mile and wished them a great race. We were able to secure a cab at the Hamilton Princess. No small feat since the roads were closing for the

Front Street Mile. We were treated to a tour of the back streets of Bermuda. We broke with our tradition to going to The Pickled Onion on Friday evening and ate at Mediterra, a new restaurant at the Fairmont. The service was impeccable. The paella and grilled swordfish, infused with flavors from the region of the Mediterranean Sea were unlike any dishes we would find in Boston. After dinner we walked around the property before settling in for the night. We meditated seated on the chairs on the balcony with the light of Gibbs Lighthouse in the distance. The door to our balcony looked like the window in the Darling house that Peter Pan used to enter the children's bedroom. The beacon from the lighthouse beckoned me to create a perfect race day in my mind's eye; to remember one of Walt Disney's favorite phrases, "It's kind of fun to do the impossible." One more day until race day.

Pre-Race Jitters   January 13, 2018

With sheer grit and determination, I made it through training. But would I make it to the starting line?

At dinner on Friday, I asked Tom how he was feeling about Sunday's race. "I am totally confident. You've got this. We're gonna have a great time."

"That's how I want to be and feel," I declared. "I want to experience that in mind, body and soul."

In my morning meditation I heard the Divine say to me again, "Why are you going to miss out on the fun?"

I knew nobody would have criticized or judged me had I chosen a DNS (did not start). People knew my story and my journey, my commitment to the sport and to my healing journey. This was my 3rd half marathon in as many years. Eleven years ago I'd been told I'd spend the rest of my life in a wheelchair and 3 years ago was told I needed a total knee replacement after a very serious knee injury. I was told to stop running. I'd already created many miracles of healing in my life.

I was in so much physical and emotional pain as I lay in bed wrestling with whether or not I was going to start my third Bermuda Half Marathon in as many years.

I knew that I am the creator of my life. By partnering with the Divine all things are possible. We went the distance in our training. I knew once I overcame myself and my fears, running feels wonderful in my body. How could I possibly rob myself of running my victory lap? I couldn't allow the fear of having collapsed at age 5 to prevail. I healed that wound at last year's Half. I'd missed out on so much fun as a child. Why was I going to miss out on the fun now?

Yet I was afraid. What if my body seized up as it had in 2017? What if my hip or back completely gave out or if anything else untoward happened in my body and I'd have to be taken off the course via ambulance? During my meditation I kept surrendering to the Divine for guidance and healing. I became aware of the roots of those thoughts and fears and then went on to remember how we created our 13.1 miles in Bermuda during all of our training runs.

I asked myself, "Are these thoughts, fears and feelings I want to carry into my future?" "No," I firmly answered. "I want to walk as my future self completely healthy, whole and healed." I had to sift and sort through all of the memories, thoughts and feelings and surrender them to the Divine for healing.

We went to the beach for the first half of the day.

I mentally rehearsed the course and talked with Tom about how amazing it was going to feel to cross the finish line.

We took the shuttle back to the hotel to have lunch by the pool. We chatted with other runners who were there for Race Weekend, and enjoyed spectacular views overlooking palm trees gently swaying from the sea breeze with the ocean in the distance. Our friend Thomas came by to see us. What a splendid reunion as we reminisced about Bermuda Marathon Weekends in past years and this weekend's festivities. We chatted poolside for a few hours and had to change plans to have an early dinner at the Jasmine Lounge. By the time we said our goodbyes and see you at the starting line, showered and were ready for dinner, all the restaurants on the property were booked. Tom and I decided we would order room service. It was perfect. We were able to get into our sweats and get ready for race day We learned that we could order breakfast to be delivered at 5:30 am. While dining on salmon, rolls, baked potatoes and hydrating with sparkling water, we watched football on TV. We drifted off to sleep after a long meditation.

I woke up as I heard the song, "A Whole New World," which is what I have my alarm set to playing softly in the background.

"It's 5:00 am Tom. It's time to get up."

"No it's not - it's only 12:20," Tom told me.

I thought it was odd that my alarm was so quiet. Tom said he heard something too.

"Well it's five o'clock somewhere," I quipped referencing Jimmy Buffett's classic song.

I was able to release a lot in a meditation. I felt incredible relief in my back as I fell back to sleep.

Until I woke up at 3:00 am....

"To change is to think greater than how we feel. To change is to act greater than the feelings of the memorized self." ~Dr. Joe Dispenza

Race Day   January 14, 2018

I woke up at 3:00 am on Sunday--race day--with my heart racing, feeling as though I was going to throw up with sweat pouring down my two arms. I don't recall whether or not I was having a dream. It was in direct contrast to how I felt when I fell back to sleep at 12:20 after the false alarm went off.

"Okay," I thought to myself. "Let's get a handle on this. Let's pull your mind out of your body and connect with the Divine. There is no time to analyze this. You have got to get to the starting line."

I reminded myself that my mind is a powerful tool and I could partner with the Divine to clear out these sensations. I went to the bathroom, came back to bed and went into a deep meditation. Mercifully I fell back to sleep. The alarm went off at 5:00 am - the real 5:00 am. We meditated for 10 minutes to set our intentions for the day. We did our core warm up and I totally trusted that room service would arrive on time. We had a 6:30 am shuttle to the starting line.

"Good morning. Good morning...Are we ready to run?"

The knock on the door came promptly at 5:30 and Narayan came in carrying a tray with everything we requested for our traditional pre-race breakfast. Tom had his piping hot coffee. We had whole wheat toast, chilled orange juice and hot water and bowls for oatmeal. We added in the bananas, nuts and granola we purchased at Miles Market.

While he organized our breakfast serving it in grand style, he said, "I am so excited for you all. I was once at base camp at Mt. Everest as support crew for a group climbing Everest. I love seeing people do epic things! Is there anything else you need?"

"No we are all set. And thank you so much!" I said.

"Of course. Have a great race day!"

I ate mindfully while letting the butterflies in my stomach just be. After breakfast, with tears in my eyes, I said a prayer for the day. I gave thanks for the blessings that brought us to that moment and asked the Divine to bless us on our 13.1 miles through Bermuda. It was intensely emotional to realize how far I'd come to be poised and ready to toe the starting line of Bermuda Half Marathon 2018 - my third in as many years.

We headed to the lobby where runners were excited to get the shuttle to the starting line. We drove through winding roads in the darkness anticipating daybreak.

When we arrived in Hamilton I saw Susan, an integral part of Bermuda Marathon Weekend along with Anthony's cousin, Jo-Ell who we met in Boston on that fateful day when Anthony offered me an invitational entry. I told Susan I had serious pre-race jitters. She took my hand and told me that it's race day excitement. It happened to her before every race.

"Why don't you use the bathrooms inside the Ferry Terminal? They're a lot better than the porta potties and then go breathe, stretch and relax. It's going to be a great day for you!"

We walked up and down Front Street going over our race strategy and remembering our previous trips to Bermuda. I reminded myself that I had two goals for the race: have fun and finish. We were blessed with another Bermudaful sunrise over Hamilton Harbor. We saw the Town Crier whose name we learned is Ed Christopher. He remembered us from the last two years and posed with us for a photo.

"Hey Denise - here they are," Lanette said.

We talked about their race strategy "To not die in the heat" and got a recap of their Front Street Mile and 10K races. This was their final leg in the Challenge with Denise running the Half and Lanette taking on the Full Marathon. After hugs and well wishes we heard the announcement. "15 minutes to the start. Runners please line up."

It was show time for Team McManus.

"Hey are you Joe Middlemiss?" I asked a tall runner wearing a Team Big Heart shirt.

"No Joey passed away and..."

"Oh I'm so sorry of course. I'm not thinking clearly. I meant to ask if you were Scott but obviously you're someone else."

"Hi I'm Linda and this is my husband Brad. How do you know about Team Big Heart?"

We were in awe of what a small world it was after I shared with them our Team Big Heart connection. We took photos of them at the starting line proudly wearing their Team Big Heart shirts and one with Ed Christopher.

We said another prayer and listened to the Town Crier make the proclamation to mark the start of the 2018 Bermuda Marathon and Half Marathon. We wished Brad and Linda a wonderful time out on the course as they were completing their Bermuda Triangle Half Challenge. After the Town Crier's proclamation, Team McManus crossed the starting line of our 13.1 adventure through Bermuda. We were not going to make the same mistake as last year of going out too fast. Tom could tell I was chomping at the bit but he made sure to be my pacer at a slow and steady pace. We ran by the Blue Waters Anglers Club and stopped at mile 1. There were a few walkers behind us but it was time to let go of thoughts of where I was in the pack. This was my race and my pace and a historic victory lap in my healing journey.

We went up the first big hill and settled into the rhythm from our training runs. We'd received so many well wishes from Facebook in the days leading up to the race. I felt everyone's energy and the energy from the Divine whisking us along. We heard the crows of the roosters. I relished the beauty and splendor of experiencing Bermuda by foot again having a deep appreciation for what it took to get me to the starting line. We did not freak out as cars passed by. We went single file and felt that we owned the road even though we were at the very very back of the pack. I knew that every step took me closer to the finish line while savoring the sensational scenery along the way. Tom made sure he was in front of me so that I didn't accelerate my pace. He could feel my nervous energy but he held an easy and steady pace. I am so happy he did. I had whispers of thoughts and feelings from when I was in a full leg brace trying to keep up with my friends. Rather than give in to those feelings as I had last year, I observed them and held myself with tenderness and compassion.

We came to the water stop around Mile 5. The volunteer and I both gasped. We met at the Front Street Mile last year and remembered each other. We hugged and chatted. Her foot is still bothering her but she has an indomitable spirit. We embraced as though we'd been dear friends for many years. She hugged Tom.

"We are having a very different race experience this year. We are taking time to enjoy every moment and make sure we pay attention to pace, hydration and fueling."

I filled her in on what happened to me last year.

"What do you need? Water, Gatorade. "Hey," she said to one of the other volunteers, "break out those orange slices for them."

"Thank you so much. You're the best!" I said.

"Here it's hot today. Take this with you."

She handed us a big bottle of water to take with us.

Back out on the course we were moving and grooving!

We passed the halfway point. What a surprise to see Jamie-Lee Wright, my earth angel from mile 12 on her bike. She asked if we needed water. Even though she couldn't run this year because of a series of injuries, she was out on the course tending to the runners. That's who and what Jamie-Lee is all about.

She took both of my hands in hers. "You look wonderful," she said. "How are you feeling?"

"I'm planning on coming into the finish vertical this year," I said with a broad smile.

Jamie-Lee smiled back and gave me a hug as she went on her way to check on other runners.

What a boost it gave me to see Jamie-Lee. Ahead of us, the locals lined the streets and cheered us along.

When you're running a Half Marathon, there is something wonderful when you hit the double digit mile mile marker especially when you're feeling awesome at mile 10! I was indeed vertical and noted that I had only 3.1 miles to go - a 5K to claim my third consecutive Bermuda Half Marathon. Tom remarked about how well I was doing even though it was hot.

"I have you to thank honey," I told him. "You made sure I kept my pace in check and didn't give into my demons."

"Hey. You know what else?" I asked.

"What?" Tom replied.

"Do you notice anything about the roads?"

"Oh my goodness," he said.

We were both on the same wavelength realizing that the roads had been paved since last year and there were no deep grooves to negotiate.

Having to walk on an uneven surface definitely contributed to last year's problems on the course. Every step to the finish line from mile 10 was an agonizing effort.

In the distance we saw the porta potties and decided to make one more stop before getting to the finish line.

Marathoners passed us and we cheered each other on.

"Good job!"

"You too!"

"You okay? You need any water?" I asked a runner who was stopped just beyond mile 10.

"No I just wish I felt better," he said as he was stretching on the side of the road.

"I'm not sure if I'm going to make it to the finish line." {Marathoners do two loops of the same course as the Half Marathoners.}

As Tom dropped behind me, I walked with him for a little while.

"Let me give you some inspiration. What's your name?"

"Joe."

"I'm Mary - from Boston. Where are you from?"

"New York"

"Do you see this wristband that says "Inspire?"

"Yes," he replied.

"Do you know why I received it?"

"No tell me," he said.

I went on to tell him my story of how I was diagnosed with Post-Polio Syndrome 11 years ago and went on to run the 2009 Boston Marathon; how 3 years ago my left knee blew out and I was told to stop running.

"I'm now just 3 miles shy of finishing my third Bermuda Half Marathon in as many years."

He was enthralled with my journey.

"Okay that's just what I needed," he said and he took off running again.

"You might see me again before the finish line," he shouted over his shoulder.

We didn't pass him again and presume he had a great finish bolstered by my story.

We kept our steady pace and paid no attention to the time on the clock. We knew we were going to finish, finish strong and finish before the last marathoner crossed the finish line. We estimated coming in at about 5 hours.

Shortly after mile 11, I heard the cheers of a volunteer with a distinct voice. He remembered the inspirational speech he gave me to help me get to the finish line when I was in distress. We joked how this year I was in much better shape than I was last year. He pointed behind us in the direction of where he was on the course when he saw me. We enjoyed a few moments together before he sent us on our way.

Last year there was no water stop after mile 12 but this year there was a spread of water and Gatorade in a bucket of ice. I took the ice and rubbed my hip and knees. We thanked the volunteers who were members of the Mid-Atlantic Athletic Club.

"You don't have far to go now," they said.

A little beyond mile 12, a family stood on their lawn with pumpkin bread in a basket.

"Would you like some pumpkin bread?" the mother asked.

We hesitated and said no thank you. She wouldn't take no for an answer. As if she knew exactly what we needed, she brought out the pumpkin bread, handed us a napkin and gave us a slice. I didn't know it was exactly what I needed until it melted in my mouth. I didn't want to have another Luna bar at mile 12 and this was the perfect fueling to get us through that final 1.1 miles.

As we turned the corner and saw the Hamilton Princess Hotel I was overcome with emotion. I remembered how much pain I was in coming into the final stretch last year and the kindness of Jamie-Lee supporting me to the finish line.

There was a detour sign and a huge hill. It took a moment for us to remember that it was the next much smaller hill we went up and down before heading into the finish.

As we approached Burnaby Street, Susan (who seemed to be everywhere) said "Up the hill and around the cones."

She paused for a moment chatting with another woman standing next to her. "You're almost there!" she said with great enthusiasm clapping her hands.

We savored the moment cheered on into the finish by Anthony's girlfriend. We had no idea the journey that would follow after receiving that invitational entry from Anthony. I felt so blessed to be coming into the finish line healthy, happy, vertical and achieving our goals of having fun and finishing the race!

We paused at the 13 mile mark to take a photo and ran strong into the finish line. The volunteers gave us our medals. We drank our cold bottles of water walking right by the medical tent this year and found Denise.

We sat down on a bench with Denise who came back to see us finish after a shower at her hotel and to wait for Lanette. We celebrated her accomplishment of completing the Bermuda Triangle Half Challenge. We sent out energy and love to Lanette who was still out on the course.

As we debriefed about the race, Denise commented, "If I would have had to go up that hill where the detour sign was, I would have died!"

We laughed as we rehydrated.

The detour sign was there for cars!

We had reservations at the Pickled Onion but I knew I wanted to get back to our hotel and recover. We were out on the course for 5 hours; the time it takes for many to run a full Marathon. I knew I needed something light to eat and to get into the pool. Denise suggested we go on our way and get a cab back to our hotel. We'd check in later. She'd keep us posted about Lanette's progress. I didn't know how I was going to walk back to the Hamilton Princess hotel to get a cab but I didn't have to. The streets surrounding the course were opened and cabs appeared out of nowhere at the corner of Front Street.

"Because crossing a finish line can be like experiencing all of life's blessings in a single moment." ~Anonymous

193

We had a delightful ride back to the hotel with a female cab driver. Since Front Street was closed, we enjoyed touring more neighborhoods we ordinarily wouldn't get to see in Bermuda. We were greeted like royalty by the Bell Staff as our taxi pulled up to the hotel. They told me to take my time as I struggled to step down out of the taxi. I was exhilarated and incredibly joyful wearing my bling. We went directly to Wickets proudly wearing our medals and chose the foods that were going to help us refuel after our triumphant 2018 Bermuda Half Marathon run. We ate Wickets Bermudian chicken salad on dark rye with chips by the pool enjoying the sunshine. After lunch we went back to our room to peel off our running clothes. It was a bit of a challenge to change my clothes with sore, stiff muscles and get into my bathing suit but getting into the pool was well worth the effort.

We were too tired to attend the after party this year. We went to Boundary Sports Bar and Grille on the grounds of the Fairmont for dinner. Wings and salads were the order of the day. To keep moving to flush out the lactic acid built up in my muscles, I started to pack up the room to get ready for our Tuesday departure. We had a football game on in the background. I fell asleep in the middle of our meditation Sunday night which I rarely do and had the deepest sleep I'd had in a very long time.

It was a full on breakfast buffet on Monday morning for me celebrating my victory. Tom enjoyed the hot breakfast throughout our stay. Except for those poppy seed muffins, I stuck to my pre-race fueling plan. I became fast friends with the omelette bar chef, Keavin, who cooked my over easy eggs to perfection. Food always tastes so wonderful after accomplishing a major goal. After breakfast we had one last trip to the beach. I needed to experience the pink sand and salty air before bracing for our return to the New England winter. The weather forecast called for rain in the afternoon. We had plans to head into Hamilton to do shopping in the afternoon.

We took showers, continued to pack and changed into going shopping and out for dinner clothes in Hamilton but first we went for one more lunch at Jasmine. Their crispy fried snapper makes my mouth water just thinking about it. It's a powerful reminder of the mind body connection in action!

While we were waiting for our food I heard someone call out, "Hey - I'm your new Facebook friend. I run with the Mystics. What's it been like two years since we met in Hyannis?"

Erik Cann was referring to that encounter we had at the Hyannis Marathon Weekend Race Expo in 2016.

Erik and I became Facebook friends through another member of the Mystics shortly before the weekend. She knew he was going to run in Bermuda. She teased him about going without the Mystics and tagged me in the post. Erik explained that he found a group of runners sharing a house for race weekend and he just had to go.

"I decided to just do it. You only live once right? I knew the other Mystics would tease me about it. Hey I'm so glad I bumped into you."

"You too. What did you think about the weekend and the race?"

"It was awesome. I'm going to definitely have to bring the Mystics with me next year."

The mist turned into downpours and we went inside to finish our last lunch in Bermuda. Our friends Shawn, and his wife, Mona, Geoff Smith and his girlfriend Allison, marathon record holder Steve Jones, and Bart Yasso and his girlfriend were seated at a large round table. We talked about our races and the weekend, asked when people were leaving and said we'd all see each other next year.

We got up early on Tuesday morning and enjoyed one last breakfast at Windows on the Sound. Keavin teased Tom that he was going to keep me in Bermuda and send Tom back to Boston; it was a typical Bermudian flirtation; one that I was very familiar with after years of hanging out with the Blue Waters Angler Club.

"By the way," Keavin said while preparing our breakfast, "did you know that Anthony and I went to high school together? Oh the stories I could tell you about that one. As a matter of fact we went out together last night. He was exhausted from the weekend."

We learned Clarence was admitted to the hospital and Anthony had no one to assist him with the weekend. That explained why we hadn't seen Clarence along the route. He recovered shortly after race weekend.

We sat by the pool where we found our fellow runners soaking up the last rays of warm sunshine before returning to our New England and Midwest destinations. We savored those final moments of being in Bermuda in January with palm trees, warm sunshine, Bermuda blue skies, bird songs and tropical flowers. As we hugged goodbye in the lobby, airport transportation shuttles arrived.

"And what team is this?" the flight attendant asked as he walked through the cabin for a pre-flight check on the return flight to Boston.

Tom and I said in unison, "Team McManus!"

"What sport is this?" he asked.

"We ran the Bermuda Half Marathon," we replied.

"That's very impressive," he commented.

As the second flight attendant prepared the cabin for take off she looked at our medals. "I don't know what you won but congratulations!"

As they brought beverage service through the cabin, we were offered complimentary beer and wine. We told them we didn't drink so they gave us extra snacks and a full can of our non-alcoholic beverage of choice. It's only an hour and a half flight between Boston and Bermuda but we had plenty of time to savor our victory.

"Good evening ladies and gentlemen. We are beginning our final descent over Boston. ..."

The sound of the Captain's voice receded into the background. As I looked out the window and saw the lights in the City below, I was reminded of how a poem I wrote in February of 2007, illuminated my way out of the dark night of my mind, body and soul.

I'm now off the sidelines, no need to sit and whine
So much gratitude fills my heart and love and beauty shine.
After all these years I can join the loving human race
I exceed all expectations and now I set the pace.

It took everything I had to train for and run the 2018 Bermuda Half Marathon. Three half marathons in as many years was quite the accomplishment for someone who was told they'd spend the rest of their life in a wheelchair; and a miracle of healing after being told in December 2014 I'd need a total knee replacement in a few years.

It's time for me to take a step back from endurance running and give my body time to heal and recover. I have total confidence in my body's ability to heal from the strain of this training cycle. I'll maintain a 5 day training cycle and go for weekly chiropractic treatments. In my meditations I will continue to experience wholeness, health and well being leaving the past behind.

Running will always be an integral part of my life and of my health and wellness regimen.

What an adventure and what a ride!

After 12 years on this healing odyssey from the effects of paralytic polio and trauma I can unequivocally say that I'm now off the sidelines. I exceeded all expectations and will continue to experience the joy in the journey on the roads and in my life.

"The cave you fear to enter holds the treasure you seek." ~Joseph Campbell

"It is by going down into the abyss that we recover the treasures of life. Where you stumble, there lies your treasure." ~Joseph Campbell

"Welcome back to Boston ladies and gentlemen. The temperature is a 'balmy' 32 degrees (the passengers laugh and groan). The time is 5:30 pm Boston time. We hope you enjoyed your flight and look forward to welcoming you back again aboard Delta Airlines."

REFERENCES AND HEALING RESOURCES

Dr. Joe Dispenza: www.drjoedispenza.com

David R. Hamilton, Ph.D.: www.drdavidhamilton.com

Jacqueline Hansen: http://www.jacquelinehansen.com/

Heal Documentary: http://www.healdocumentary.com/

Mary McManus:
www.marymcmanus.com
www.youtube.com/marysunshine100
www.adventuresrunnergirl.blogspot.com

Billy Mills: https://www.youtube.com/watch?v=DfLLNksZmoY

Anita Moorjani: https://anitamoorjani.com/

Patti Penn: https://www.pauseinjoy.com/

Candace Pert: http://candacepert.com/

Bill Rodgers: http://www.billrodgersrunningcenter.com/

Bernie Siegel, MD: http://www.berniesiegelmd.com

Lizzie Sobel, DC www.wholesomehealingchiro.com

What the bleep do we know?: https://whatthebleep.com

Bart Yasso: www.bartyasso.com

Mary McManus was once known as "Easy Out Alper in gym class. She contracted paralytic polio at the age of 5 but managed to run the 2009 Boston Marathon at the age of 55. When Mary was diagnosed with Post-Polio Syndrome, a progressive neuromuscular disease in December 2006, she decided she was not going to take the diagnosis sitting down. In May 2007, Mary took a leap of faith leaving behind her award winning career as a Social Worker at the VA to heal her life. She got still and asked for Divine Guidance. The answer came in the form of a poem, "Running the Race" followed by many poems that, through the power of visualization, inspired her to heal mind, body and soul. Mary's quest to heal her life led her to the sport of running that tested her mettle while fueling her journey of transformation from a survivor of childhood paralytic polio and severe trauma at the hands of family members to a woman who embodies faith, grace under fire, courage, determination, endurance and resilience.

"Running the Race" foreshadowed her Boston Marathon run despite all appearances to the contrary. As Mary sat in a leg brace, using a cane and a wheelchair for mobility, and having been told to prepare to spend the rest of her life in a wheelchair, Mary imagined herself winning a 10K race. Out of the rubble of her past, Mary dug deep to discover the treasure of who she was always meant to be. Her Spirit shines with brilliant resilience as she conquered every challenge going the distance on the roads and in her life.

Mary holds a BS in Communications from Boston University, an MSW from Boston College and many fond memories of her veterans and their families who blessed her life when she worked at the VA. She lives in Chestnut Hill Massachusetts with Tom, her husband of over 40 years, and their beloved cat Jamie.

Photo credits:
Front Cover Photo: Johannes Hirn, Ph.D.
April 20, 2009

Back Cover Photo: Michael Marsili
Davis Hairdressing Salon
South Boston, MA
December 2018

Rave review for "The Adventures of Runnergirl 1953:

"A most unlikely runner stood to my right as I gave the oral command for the mobility impaired start of the 113th Boston Marathon on April 20, 2009. That most unlikely runner was Mary McManus. She overcame the childhood challenges of paralytic polio and years of childhood trauma to become a runner at the age of 53 years old and take on the challenge of the Boston Marathon at 55 years old. In "The Adventures of Runnergirl 1953" you'll be inspired as I have been by her courage, resilience and determination to overcome whatever obstacles life put in her path. Mary's life story set against the backdrop of running in "The Adventures of Runnergirl 1953" will leave you asking the question, "If Mary was able to accomplish all that in the face of seemingly overwhelming odds, what's stopping me from being the best I can be?"

Dave McGillivray
Race Director – B.A.A. Boston Marathon

36794174R00125

Made in the USA
Middletown, DE
18 February 2019